Jennifer Williams trained as a domestic science (home economics) teacher but her interest in textile crafts started when she was only six years old. Her tatting designs have been published in tatting and lace magazines and are displayed at various textile and lace exhibitions. Jennifer is a member of the international guild, the Ring of Tatters. Jennifer is based in Oxfordshire, UK. Visit her website for patterns and technique tutorials:

www.cariad-tatting.com

The original best-selling Twenty to Make *series has sold over 2 million copies worldwide! Each book in this new series is published in hardback pocket-size format, making them perfect little gifts.*

Like this book? Here are some more in this series:

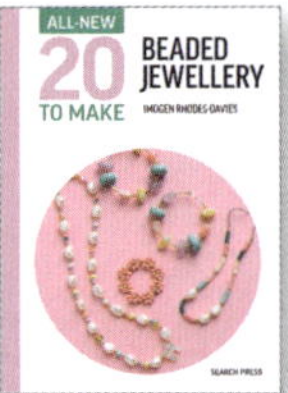

9781800922587   9781800922518   9781800920989   9781800921467

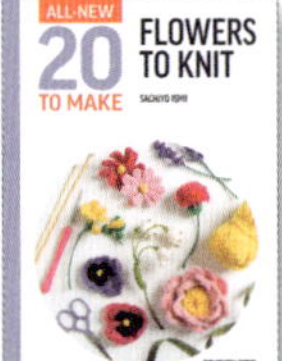

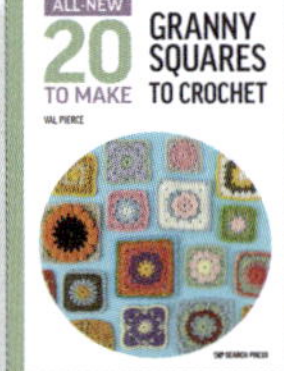

9781800920873   9781800921399   9781800921009   9781800923553

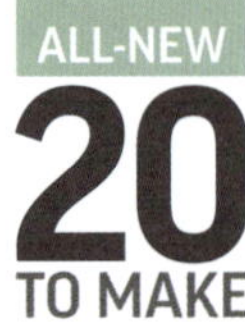

To discover the full range of titles in the *All-New 20 to Make* series, scan the QR code, right or visit www.searchpress.com

ALL-NEW 20 TO MAKE

TATTED SNOWFLAKES

Jennifer Williams

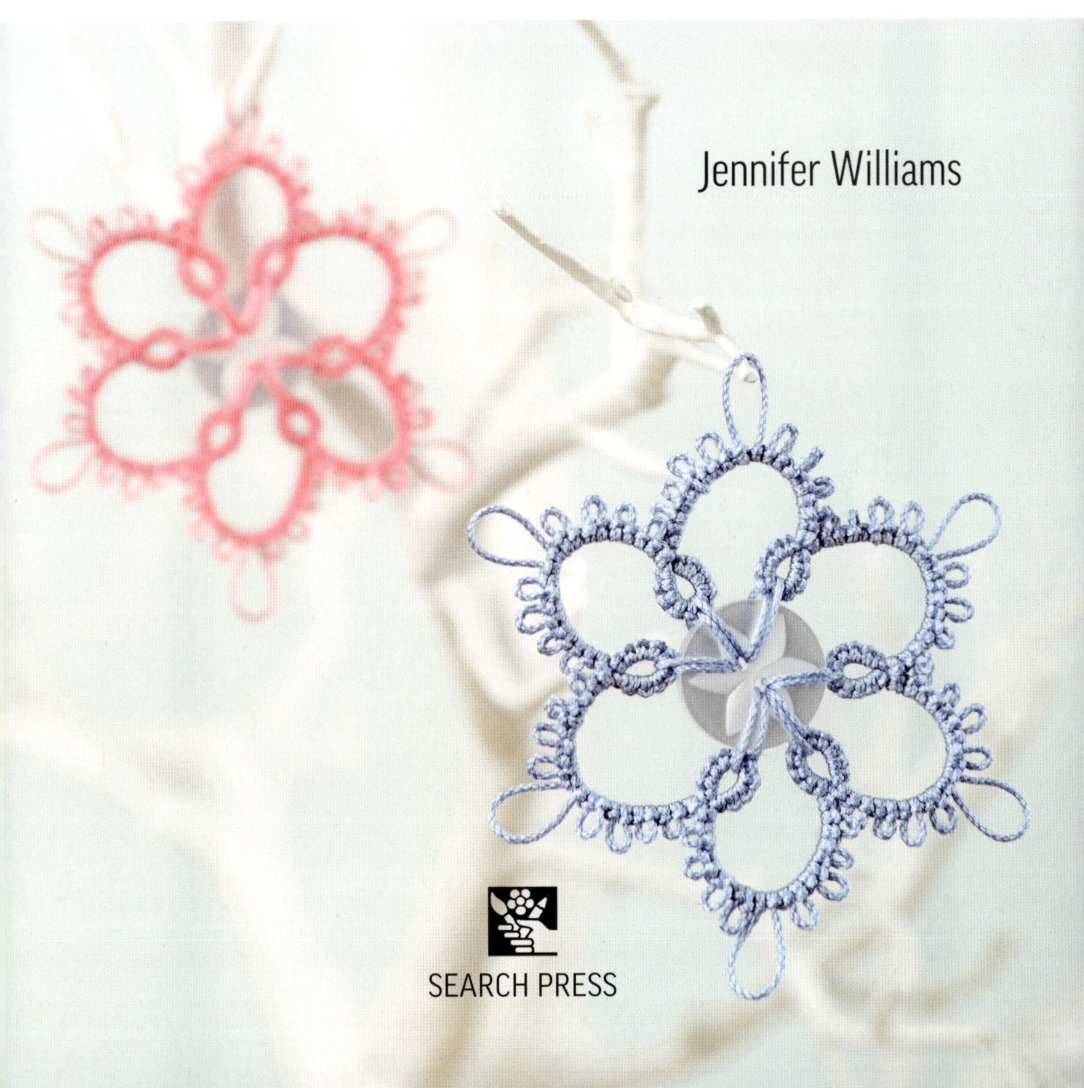

SEARCH PRESS

This edition published in 2026
Search Press Limited
Wellwood, North Farm Road
Tunbridge Wells, Kent TN2 3DR

Originally published in 2015

1 2 3 4 5 6 7 8 9 10

ISBN: 978-1-80092-330-0
ebook ISBN: 978-1-80093-317-0

Bookmarked Hub
For further ideas and inspiration, and to join our free online
community, visit www.bookmarkedhub.com

Publishers' notes
Metric measurements are used in this book; the imperial
conversions are rounded to the nearest 1/16in. Always use
either metric or imperial measurements, not a combination
of both.

The Publishers and author can accept no responsibility for
any consequences arising from the information, advice or
instructions given in this publication.

For errata, please visit our website (www.searchpress.com) or
the Bookmarked Hub (www.bookmarkedhub.com).

GPSR information can be found at www.searchpress.com
Printed in China, AP032026

DEDICATION

To my children for their encouragement and support.

CONTENTS

PROJECTS

INTRODUCTION

Snowflakes are usually associated with winter and we copy their delicate shapes to make tree decorations and embellishments to go on Christmas cards. However, the snowflake shape is too pretty to be confined to just this time of year and looks beautiful worked in different shades, with coloured beads or sequins.

Tatted snowflakes can be used in many ways: to hang in windows, on Christmas trees or to decorate a greetings card, for example. I have used the designs in this book to embellish some gloves, a tealight holder and a scarf, and I have made one of them into a pendant and earrings set.

The patterns are suitable for tatters with just the basic tatting skills because explanations for any other techniques are incorporated in the instructions. Some useful techniques can be found on pages 10 and 11.

Most of the designs are tatted without the addition of any embellishments, but I have added beads to others to give them a different dimension, and a bit of 'bling'. The beads used are mostly round seed or 4mm (³⁄₁₆in) beads but I have also used drop beads, which are pear-shaped. The designs named Anne (page 58) and Karen (page 24) have large sequins, which are known as 'spangles', enclosed between two tatted circles at their centres, and Karen has small sequins on the tatted chains as well.

Arwenna (page 43) and Hannah (page 34) incorporate small buttons and Lynn (page 49) and Eileen (page 52) have been tatted onto small plastic curtain rings.

I really enjoyed designing these snowflakes and I hope you will have fun tatting them.

Jennifer

To see more of Jennifer's designs and for help with tatting techniques, visit:

www.cariad-tatting.com

Tatting is a very portable craft requiring as little equipment as a shuttle, small crochet hook, scissors, thread and a pattern. You can include another shuttle or two, beads, needles to string the beads and to sew in the ends on your finished pieces, a very fine crochet hook and jewellery findings.

THREAD

The designs in this book have been tatted using size 20 or 10 crochet cotton, but you can tat with any thickness of thread provided it is smooth. For best results, use the thread that is stipulated in the pattern.

CROCHET HOOK

A small size 0.75mm (US 13) steel hook is used to draw a loop through a picot on another element of your tatting so that you can make a join. A fine hook (size 0.4mm/US 16) is used to add beads to picots, before working a join, and also to add just a few beads to the thread.

PICOT GAUGES

I use the following items as picot gauges:

- An unfolded paper clip
- A coffee stirrer
- A cocktail stick

SHUTTLES

These can be made from wood, metal, bone and horn, but are usually plastic, as shown on page 7 (bottom, right). Some have a removable spool in the centre to hold the thread, while others have a 'post' in the centre, round which to wind the thread. Shuttles are pointed at both ends, so look boat-shaped, or they can have a metal hook added to one end. Other shuttles have an extension at one end forming a 'pick' which is used, like the hook, to make joins between two elements of tatting.

NEEDLES

- Long beading needles are used in conjunction with a fine sewing thread for stringing beads.

- Size 18 or 16 tapestry needles are used for sewing in loose ends of thread, to hide them, when you have finished your piece of tatting.

- Big-eyed needles are split from end to end, so are very useful when stringing beads on any thickness of thread.

ABBREVIATIONS

+	join
B	bead, so 3B = three beads
Beaded dpb/ beaded dpf	dropped picot with 1 or 3 beads in place of the 'picot'
CH.	chain
cl	close ring
CTM	continuous thread method
DNRW	do not reverse work
dpb	dropped picot to the back: 3 second half stitches, picot or bead, 3 first half stitches
dpf	dropped picot to the front: 3 first half stitches, picot or bead, 3 second half stitches
ds	double stitch: this is usually omitted and the pattern has just the number of double stitches to be worked
JR.	Josephine ring (a double stitch followed by a number, usually 12, second half stitches)
LC	lock chain (turn the first half of the double stitch as usual, but do not turn the second half of the double stitch)
Lp	large picot: 1cm (½in) open measurement; use a coffee stirrer or short double-ended 3.25mm (US 3) knitting needle
mp	medium picot: 7mm (¼in) open measurement; use a cocktail stick as a picot gauge
MR.	mock ring
p	picot: open measurement 5mm (¼in); use an unfolded paper clip as a picot gauge
R.	ring
RW	reverse work
SH.1	shuttle 1
sj	shuttle join
SLT	Shoelace Trick (make an overhand tie so that the threads change place)
sms	small sequin
SS	swap shuttles
Tension	to push the double stitches close together, or spread them out, in order to make a chain curve
vbp	very big picot: 2cm (¾in) open measurement; use a pencil or similar as a picot gauge
vsp	very small picot: just big enough to insert a size 0.75mm (US 13) crochet hook

TECHNIQUES

SHUTTLE JOIN

This type of join is used when the working shuttle thread is nearer to the picot, or small space, to which the join is to be made, than the auxiliary (ball) thread.

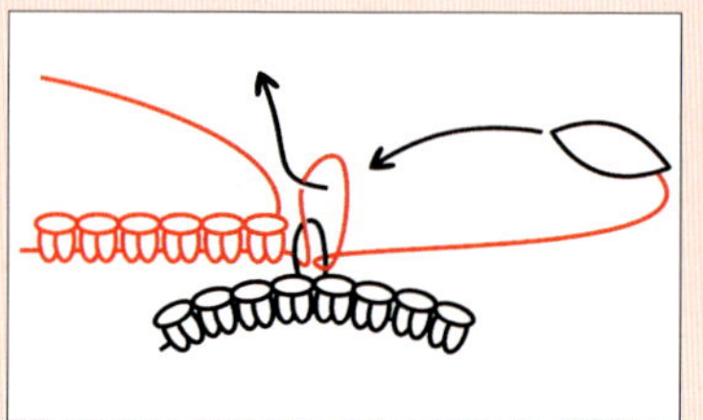

1 Draw a loop in the shuttle thread up through the picot, or small space, indicated in the pattern.

2 Pass the shuttle through this loop, then adjust the threads to bring the previous stitches close to the join.

3 Pull the shuttle to close the join.

PICOT GAUGE

Where used in this book, the picot gauge is held parallel to the core thread.

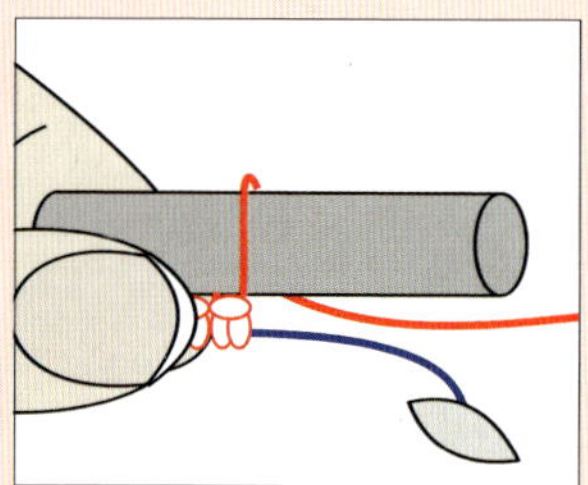 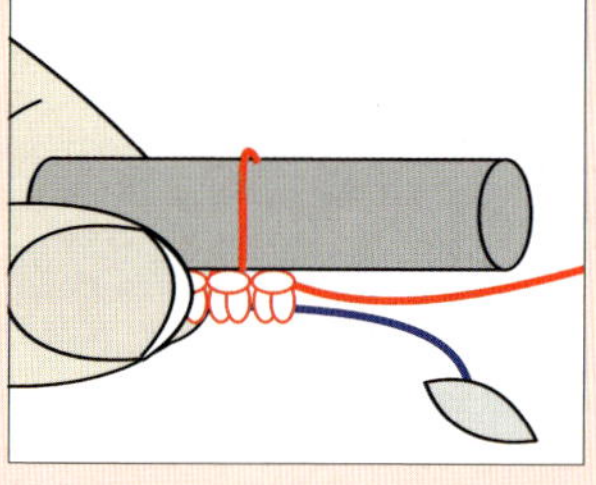

1 The thread from your hand goes up and over to the back of the picot gauge.

2 Work the following stitch next to the double stitch before the picot.

FOLDED JOIN

This technique helps you join the last ring to the first ring in a design.

1 Work the final ring as far as the join.

2 Fold the motif away from you, bringing the first ring in place behind your work and matching it up with the final ring.

3 Insert a crochet hook through the picot that you wish to join to from the back.

4 Hook the working thread (the one round your hand, not the shuttle thread) and draw a loop through the joining picot.

5 Pass the shuttle through the loop from front to back. Make sure the loop has not twisted.

6 Adjust the threads as for a normal join, then work a second half stitch.

7 Complete the ring according to the pattern.

8 Here's the finished snowflake showing the completed join.

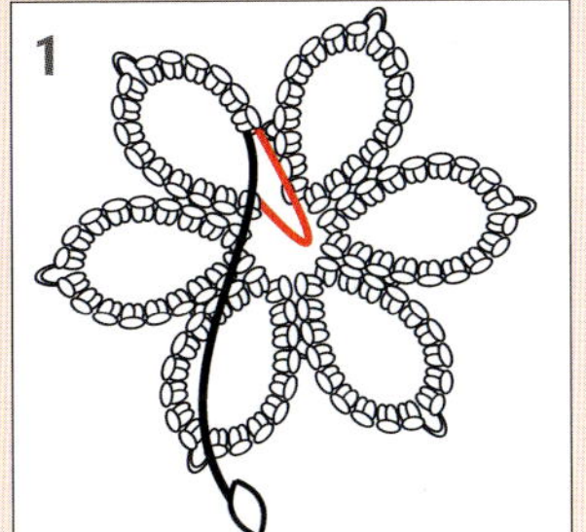

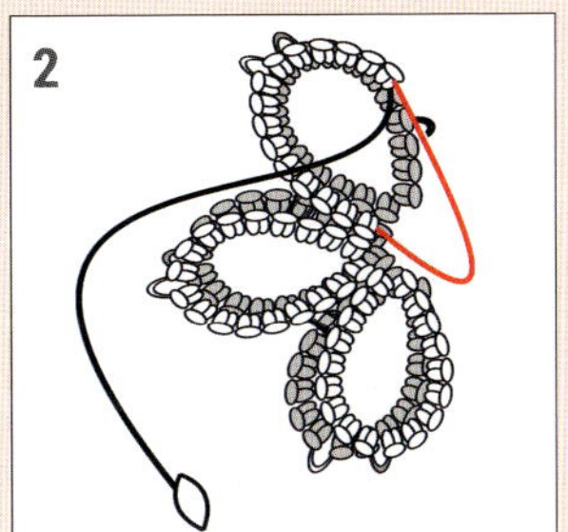

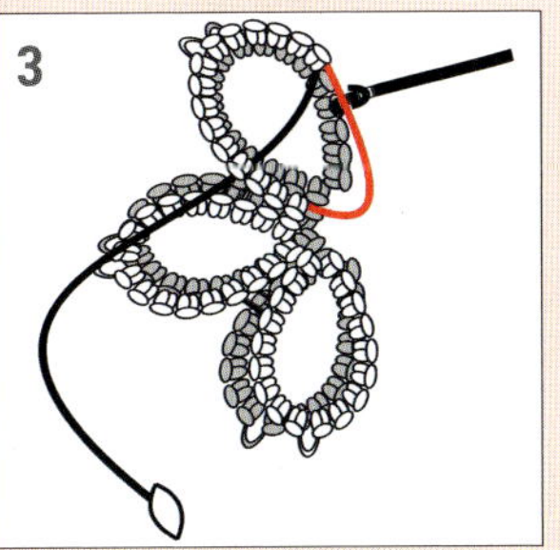

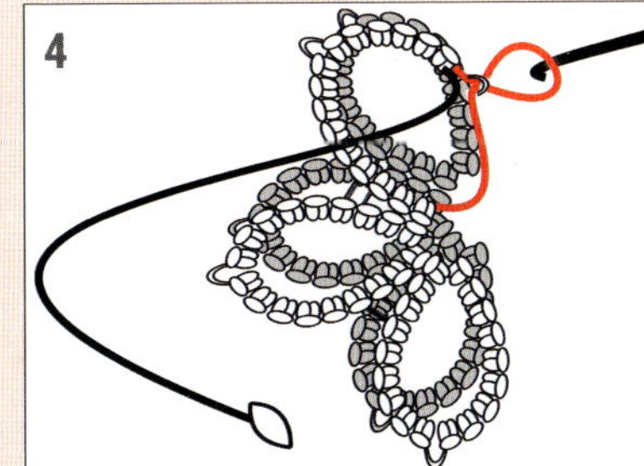

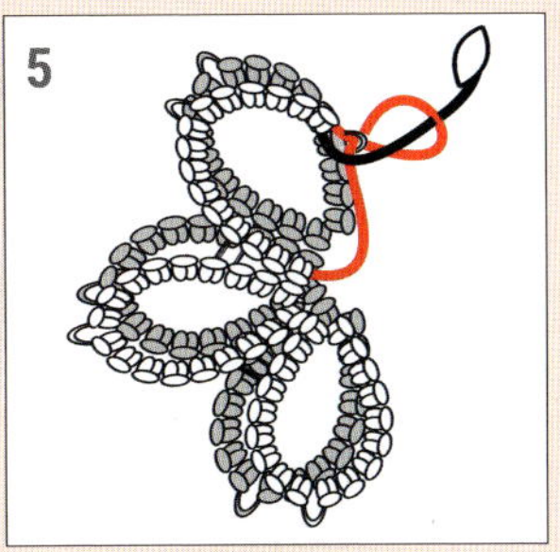

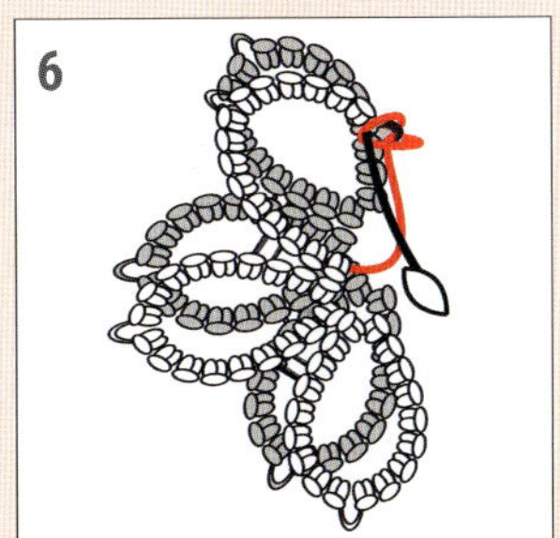

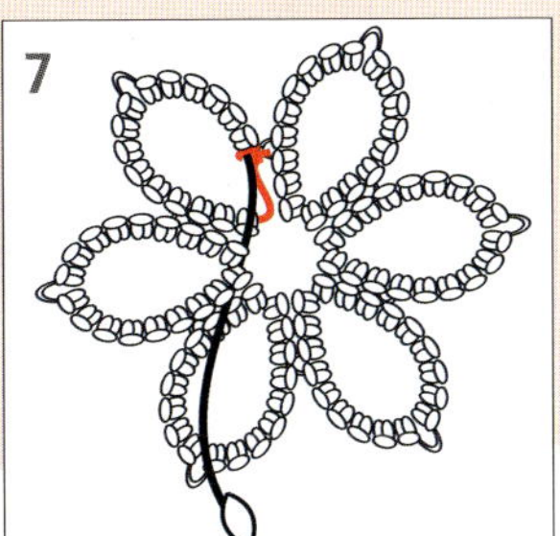

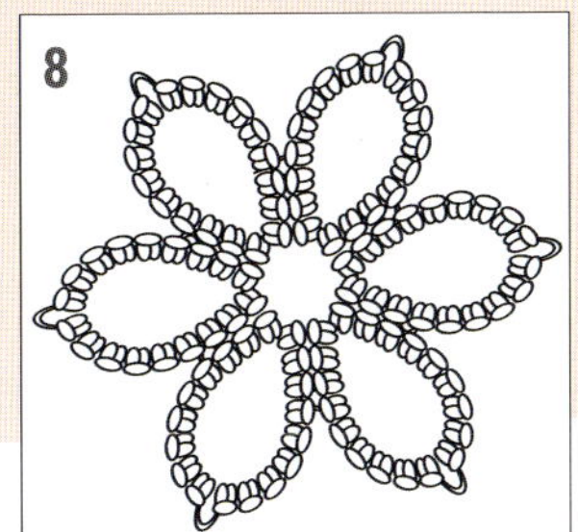

PROJECTS

ALISON

YOU WILL NEED

- Size 20 thread
- 2 x shuttles
- Crochet hook, 0.75mm (US 13)
- Small pair of scissors

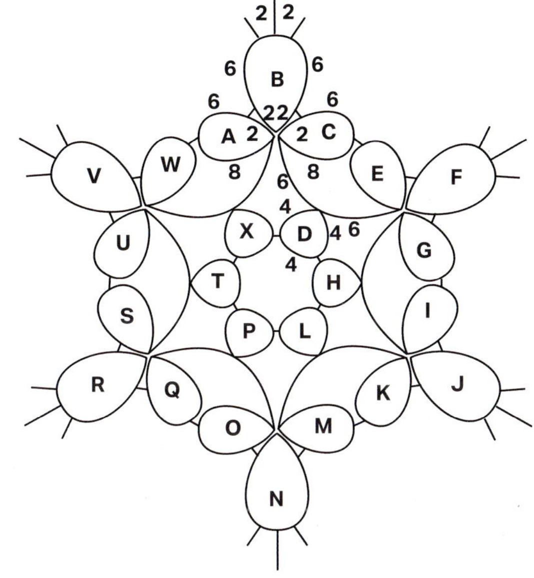

INSTRUCTIONS

Wind two shuttles CTM with 5m (5½yd) of thread onto shuttle 1 and 2.5m (2¾yd)
onto shuttle 2.

SH.1	R.A	8, p, 6, p, 2, cl
	R.B	2, + to previous ring, 6, mp, 2, Lp, 2, mp, 6, p, 2, cl
	R.C	2, + to previous ring, 6, p, 8, cl, RW
	CH.	6, SS, DNRW

SH.2	R.D	4, p, 4, p, 4, cl, SS, DNRW

SH.1	CH.	6, RW

	*R.E	8, + to last ring on previous three-ring group, 6, p, 2, cl
	R.F	2, + to previous ring, 6, mp, 2, Lp, 2, mp, 6, p, 2, cl
	R.G	2, + to previous ring, 6, p, 8, cl, RW
	CH.	6, SS, DNRW

SH.2	R.H	4, + to previous ring off chain, 4, p, 4, cl, SS, DNRW

SH.1	CH.	6, RW**

Repeat from * to ** four times, remembering to join ring W to ring A and ring X to
ring D on the last repeat (see diagram).

Cut and tie to the base of rings A, B and C. Secure all the ends. Block and stiffen
as required.

AURIEL

YOU WILL NEED

- Size 20 thread
- Shuttle
- Crochet hook, 0.75mm (US 13)
- Small pair of scissors
- 3 x picot gauges graded in size – for example, an unfolded paper clip for 'p'; a cocktail stick for 'mp'; and a short size 3.25mm (US 3) double-ended knitting needle for 'Lp'

INSTRUCTIONS
ROW 1 (SEE DIAGRAM 1)

Wind about 2.5m (2¾yd) onto the shuttle. Do not cut.

R.A	6, p, 3, p, 6, cl
R.B	6, p, 3, p, 6, cl, RW
CH.	5, p, 5, RW
*R.C	6, + to previous ring, 3, p, 6, cl
R.D	6, p, 3, p, 6, cl, RW

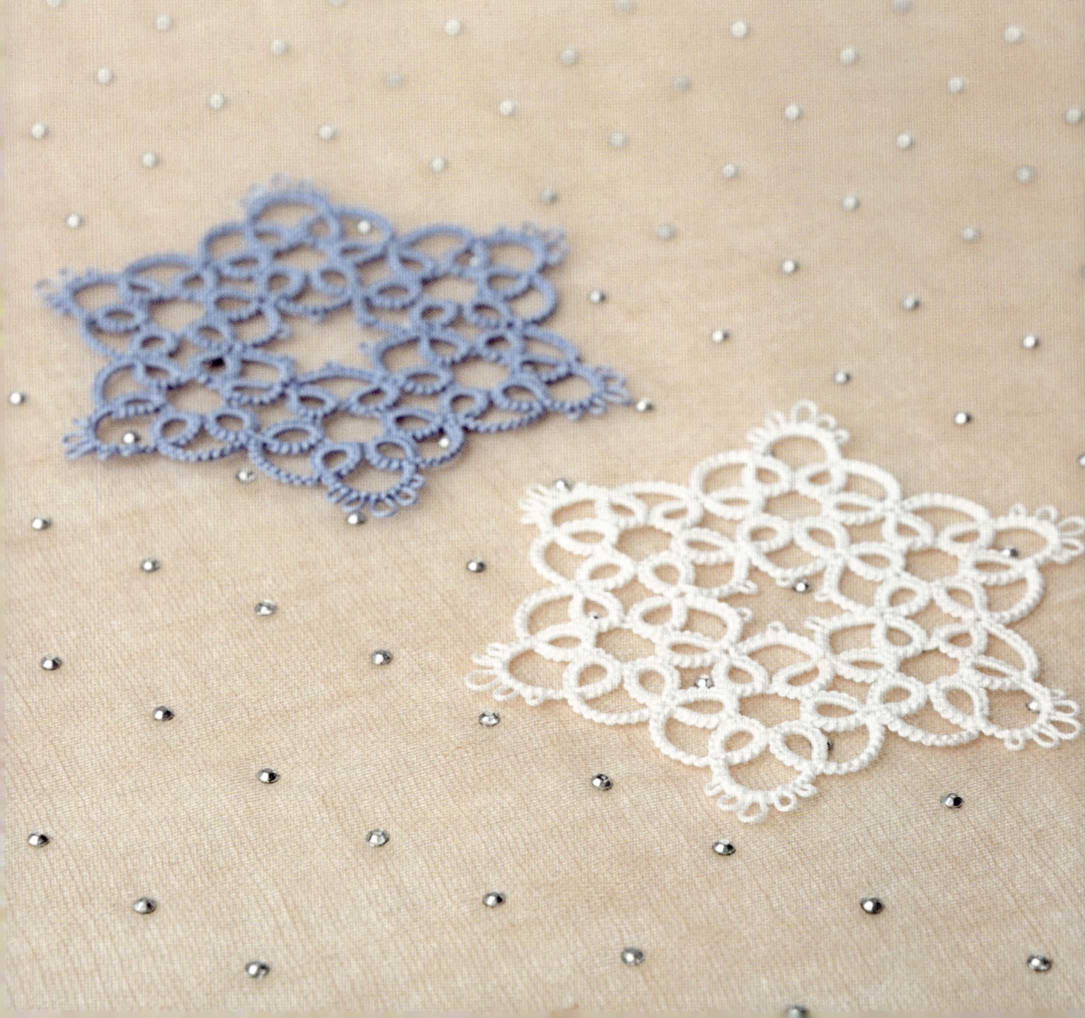

CH.   5, p, 5**

Repeat from * to ** three more times, then:

R.K   6, + to previous ring, 3, p, 6, cl

R.L   6, p, 3, + to ring A, 6, cl, RW

CH.   5, p, 5

Cut and tie to the base of rings A and B then secure the ends.

ROW 2 (SEE DIAGRAMS 2 AND 3)

Wind about 4m (4½yd) of thread onto the shuttle. Do not cut.

R.A   6, p, 3, + to the left-hand ring of one of the two ring groups on row 1, 6, cl

R.B   6, + to the right hand ring of the same two ring groups on row 1, 3, p, 6, cl, RW

CH.   10, tension, RW

R.C   6, + to ring B, 3, p, 6, cl, RW

CH.   3, p, 2, mp, 2, Lp, 2, mp, 2, p, 3, tension, RW

R.D   6, + to ring C, 3, p, 6, cl, RW

CH.   10, tension, RW

*R.E   6, + to previous ring, 3, + to the adjacent ring on row 1, 6, cl

R.F   6, + to the adjacent ring on row 1, 3, p, 6, cl, RW

CH.   10, tension, RW

R.G   6, + to previous ring, 3, p, 6, cl, RW

CH.   3, p, 2, mp, 2, Lp, 2, mp, 2, p, 3, tension, RW#

R.H   6, + to previous ring, 3, p, 6, cl, RW

CH.   10, tension, RW**

Repeat from * to ** three more times, then repeat from * to # and continue:

R.X   6, + to ring W, 3, + to ring A, 6, cl, RW

CH.   10, tension

Cut and tie to the base of rings A and B then secure the ends. Block and stiffen as required.

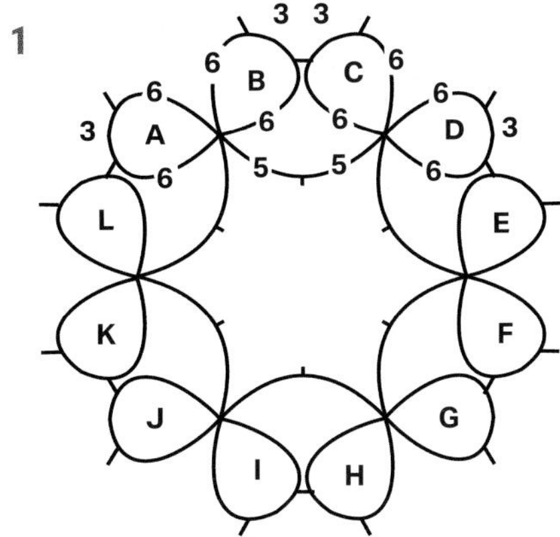

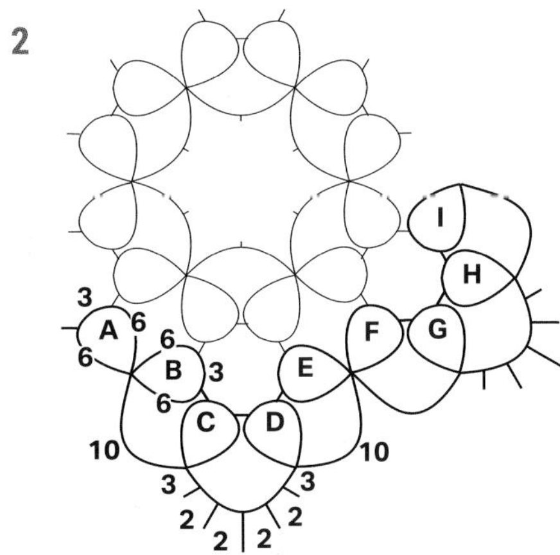

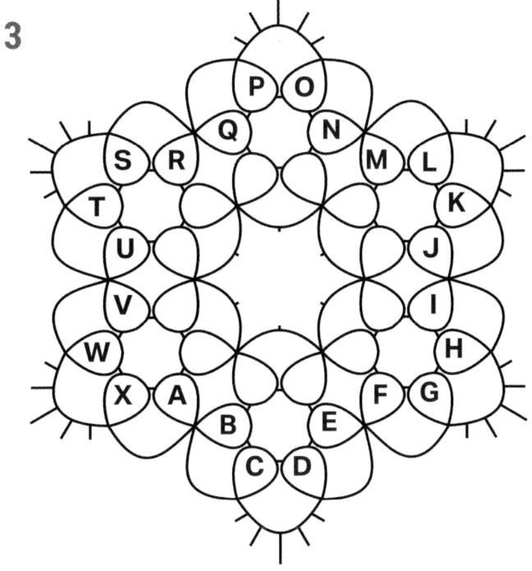

HELEN

YOU WILL NEED

- Size 20 thread
- Shuttle
- Crochet hook, 0.4mm (US 16)
- Small pair of scissors
- 66 x size 11 beads

INSTRUCTIONS

ROW 1 (SEE DIAGRAM 1)

String 6 of the beads then wind about 1.5m (1¾yd) of thread onto the shuttle, leaving the beads on the ball thread.

R.A   4, p, 4, p, 4, p, 4, cl, RW

CH.   2, B, 2, RW

*R.B   4, p, 4, p, 4, p, 4, cl, RW

CH.   2, B, 2, RW**

Repeat from * to ** four more times.

Cut and tie to the base of ring A then secure the ends.

ROW 2

String 54 beads then wind about 4.5m (5yd) of thread onto the shuttle along with the beads.

R.G   Bring 1 bead (from the shuttle) into the ring round your hand:
8, B, 5, p, 3, cl (see diagram 2)

R.H   Bring 7 beads (from the shuttle) into the ring round your hand:
3, + to ring G, 3, B, 2, B, 2, 3B, 2, B, 2, B, 3, p, 3, cl

R.I   Bring 1 bead (from the shuttle) into the ring round your hand:
3, + to ring H, 5, B, 8, cl, RW

LC.   8, add a bead (using the fine crochet hook) to the middle picot on one of the rings on row 1, 8, RW

*R.J   Bring 1 bead (from the shuttle) into the ring round your hand:
8, B, 5, p, 3, cl (see diagram 3)

R.K   Bring 7 beads (from the shuttle) into the ring round your hand:
3, + to previous ring, 3, B, 2, B, 2, 3B, 2, B, 2, B, 3, p, 3, cl

R.L   Bring 1 bead (from the shuttle) into the ring round your hand:
3, + to previous ring, 5, B, 8, cl, RW

LC.   8, add a bead (using the fine crochet hook) to the middle picot on the adjacent ring on row 1, 8, RW**

Repeat from * to ** four more times (see diagram 4), then cut and tie to the base of rings G, H and I. Secure the ends.

Block and stiffen as required.

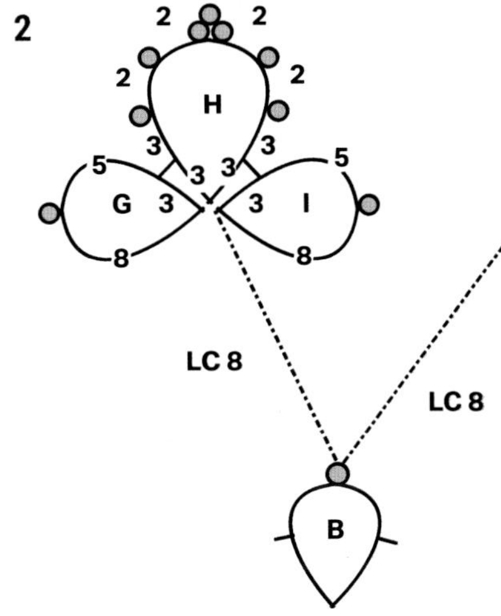

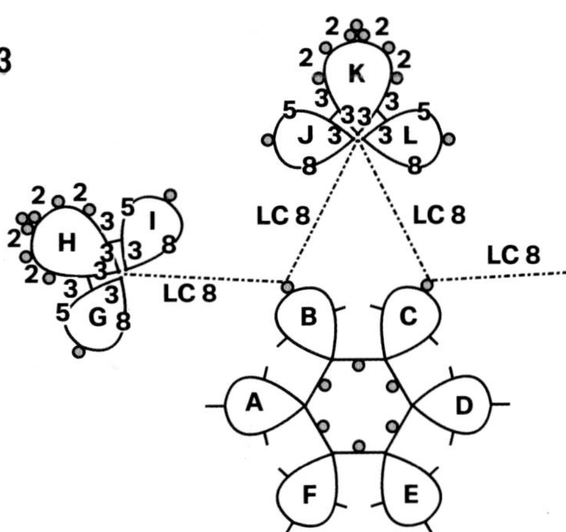

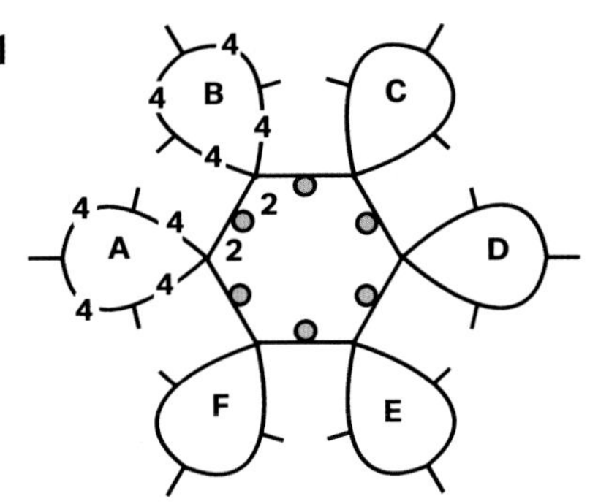

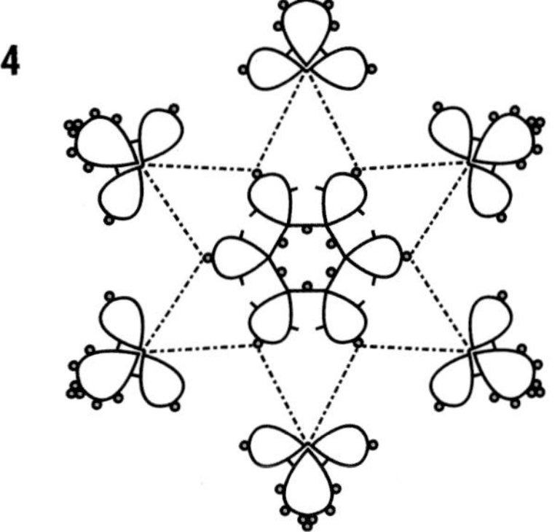

GILLIAN

YOU WILL NEED

- Size 20 thread
- Shuttle
- Crochet hook, 0.75mm (US 13)
- Small pair of scissors
- 42 x size 11 beads

INSTRUCTIONS

String 42 beads then wind about 1.5m (1¾yd) of thread onto the shuttle along with 6 of the beads. Do not cut.

ROW 1

R.A   Bring 6 beads into the ring round your hand:
6, 6B, 6, cl, RW

CH.   6, 3B, 6, RW (see diagram 1)

*R.B   6, move 1 of the beads on ring A to the left then + to the picot, 6, cl, RW

CH.   6, 3B, 6, cl, RW** (see diagram 2)

Repeat from * to ** four more times but do not reverse work after the fourth repeat.

Work a sj into the base of ring A (see diagram 3).

Do not cut.

ROW 2

CH.   8, 3B, 8, sj into the base of the adjacent ring

Repeat this chain five more times, omitting the final shuttle join, then cut and tie to the base of ring A (see diagram 4).

Block and stiffen as required.

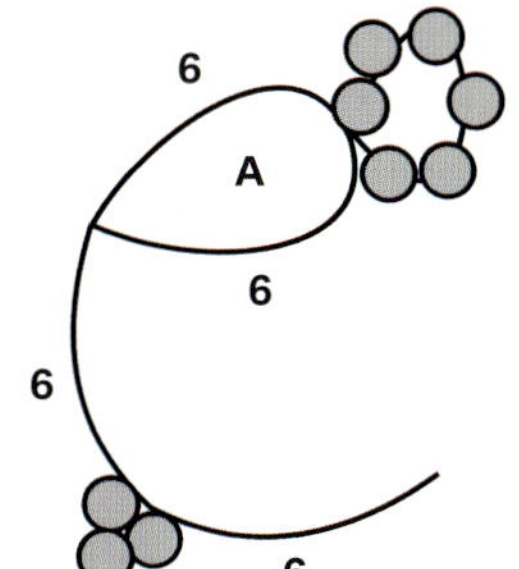

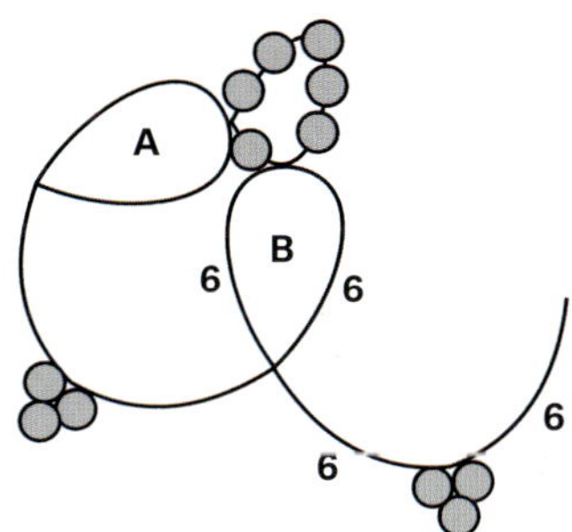

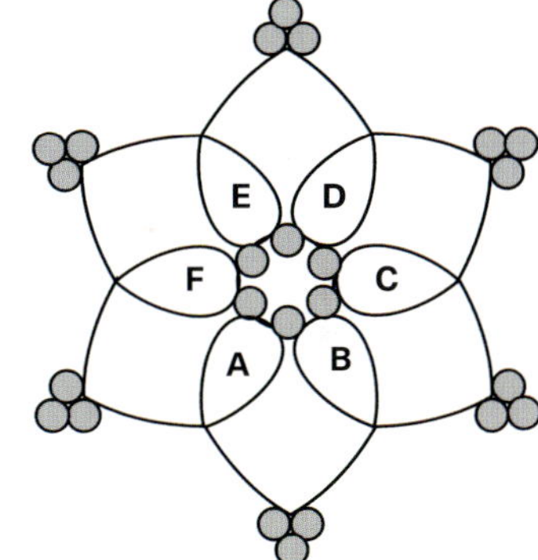

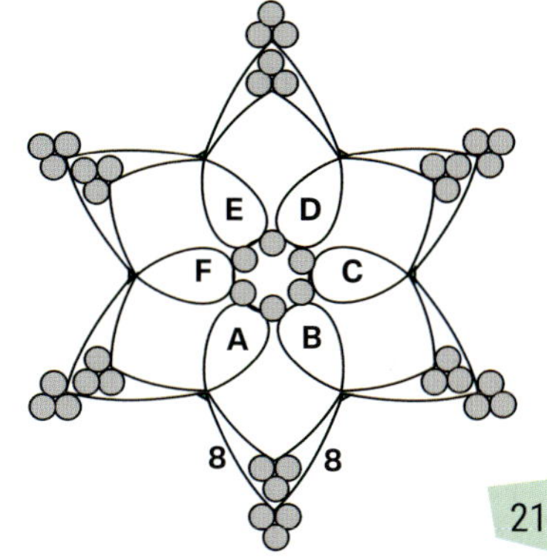

CATRIN

YOU WILL NEED

- Size 20 thread
- Shuttle
- Crochet hook, 0.75mm (US 13)
- Small pair of scissors
- Tapestry needle

INSTRUCTIONS

ROW 1

Wind about 1.5m (1⅝yd) of thread onto the shuttle.
Do not cut (see diagram 1).

R.A   2, (p, 2) x 5, cl, RW

CH.   18, tension to measure 2cm (¾in), RW

*R.B   2, p, 2, + to the fourth picot on the previous ring,
2, (p, 2) x 3, cl, RW

CH.   18, tension to measure 2cm (¾in), RW**

Repeat from * to ** three more times, then:

R.F   2, p, 2, + to the second free picot on ring E, 2, p, 2,
        join to the middle free picot on ring A, 2, p, 2, cl, RW

CH.   18, tension to measure 2cm (¾in)

Cut and tie to the base of ring A then secure the ends.

ROW 2

Wind about 3.5m (3¾yd) of thread onto the shuttle.
Do not cut.

*R.G   6, p, 4, p, 2, cl

R.H   2, + to previous ring, 4, (p, 2) x 4, p, 4, p, 2, cl (see
        diagram 2)

R.I   2, + to previous ring, 4, p, 6, cl, RW

CH.   22, tension to measure 2cm (¾in), RW**

Repeat from * to ** five more times.

Cut and tie to the base of rings G, H and I, then secure the
ends (see diagram 3).

ASSEMBLING THE SNOWFLAKE

Place row 1 inside row 2 (see diagam 4), then draw each of
the three ring groups, in turn, through the chains on row 1
(see diagram 5). Block and stiffen as required.

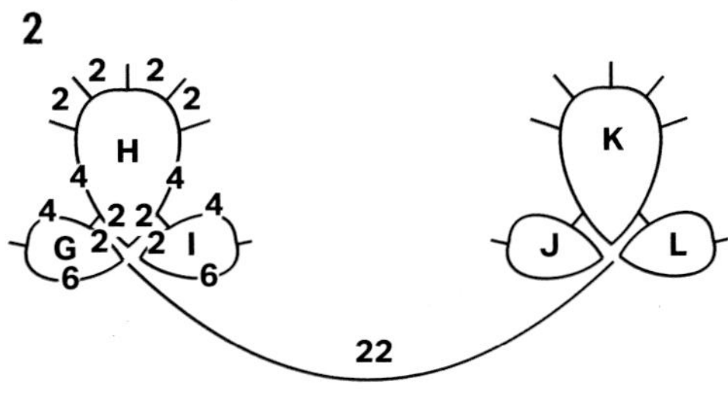

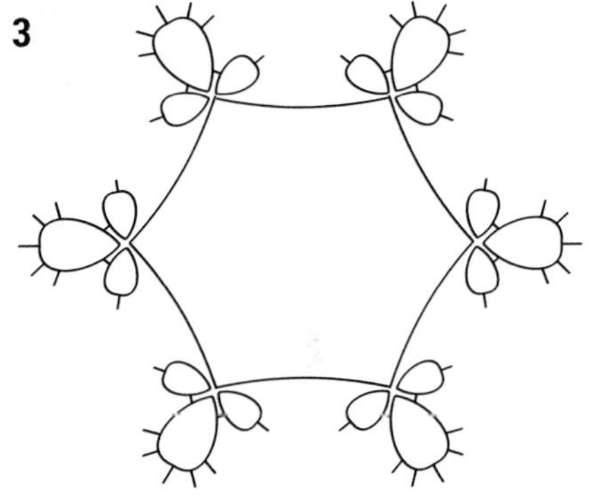

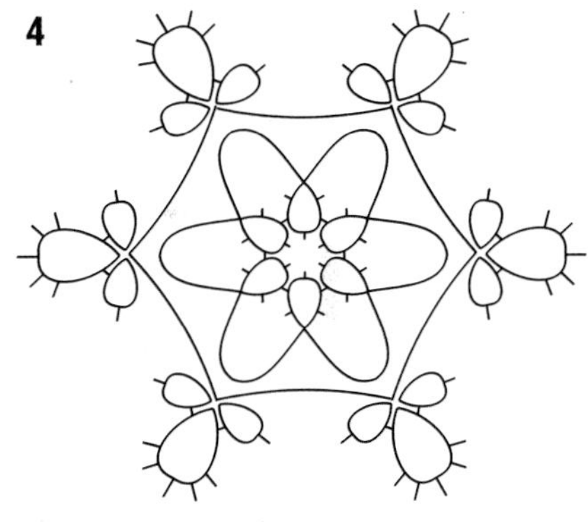

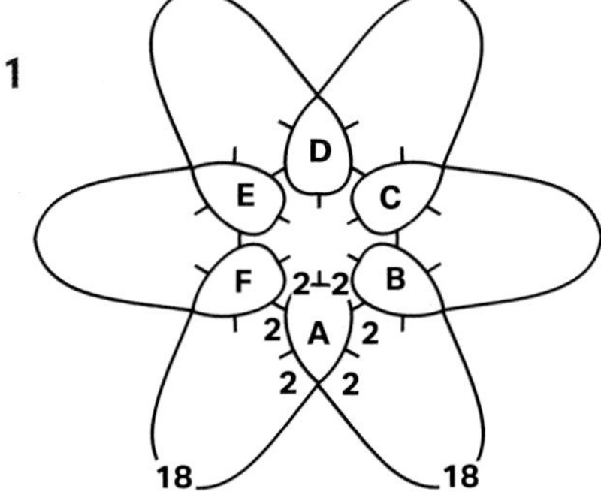

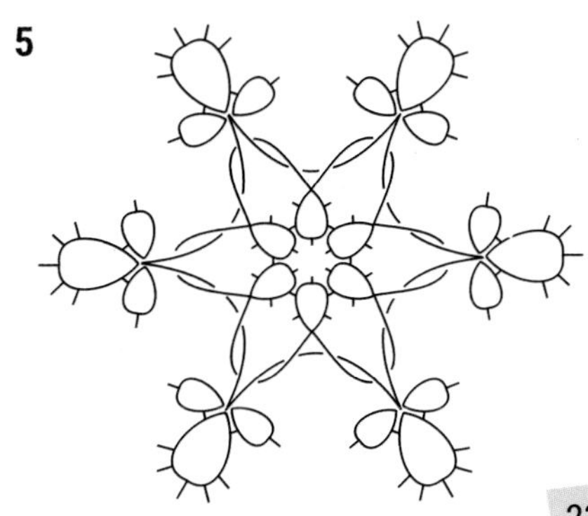

KAREN

YOU WILL NEED

- Size 20 thread
- Shuttle
- 2 x crochet hooks, 0.75mm and 0.4mm (US 13 and 16)
- Small pair of scissors
- Big-eyed needle or beading needle
- 2cm (¾in) sequin or disc
- 48 x small sequins

INSTRUCTIONS

ROW 1 (SEE DIAGRAM 1)

Wind about 1.25m (1½yd) of thread onto the shuttle. Do not cut.

R.A	6, p, 2, p, 6, cl, RW
CH.	4, + sms, 4, RW
R.B	6, + (to second 'p' on previous ring), 2, p, 6, cl, RW
CH.	4, + sms, 4, RW
*R.C	6, + (to 'p' on previous ring), 2, p, 6, cl, RW
CH.	4, + sms, 4, RW

Repeat from * twice more (5 rings and chains).

R.F	6, + (to 'p' on previous ring), 2, + (to picot on ring A), 6, cl, RW
CH.	4, + sms, 4

Cut and tie to the base of ring A.

ROW 2 (SEE DIAGRAM 2)

Wind about 1.25m (1⅜yd) of thread onto the shuttle.
Do not cut.

R.A   6, p, 2, p, 6, cl, RW

CH.   6, + sms, 4, sms, 6, RW

R.B   6, + (to second 'p' on previous ring), 2, p, 6, cl, RW

CH.   6, + sms, 4, sms, 6, RW

*R.C   6, + (to 'p' on previous ring), 2, p, 6, cl, RW

CH.   6, + sms, 4, sms, 6, RW

Repeat from * twice more (5 rings and chains).

R.F   6, + (to 'p' on previous ring), 2, + (to picot on ring A), 6, cl, RW

CH.   6, + sms, 4, sms, 6

Cut and tie to the base of ring A.

ROW 3 (SEE DIAGRAMS 3 AND 4)

Wind about 2m (2¼yd) of thread onto the shuttle.
Do not cut.

Place row 1 on top of row 2, lining up the rings.

R.A   8, + to the base of ring A on row 1 and the base of ring A on row 2 together, 8, cl, RW

CH.   5, (+ sms, 4) x 4, sms, 5, RW

*R.B   8, + to the base of the adjacent ring on row 1 and the base of the adjacent ring on row 2 together, 8, cl, RW

CH.   5, (+ sms, 4) x 4, sms, 5, RW**

Repeat from * to ** to the end of row, remembering to slip the large sequin in between rows 1 and 2 before joining the fifth ring. Cut and tie to the base of ring A.

Block and stiffen as required.

1

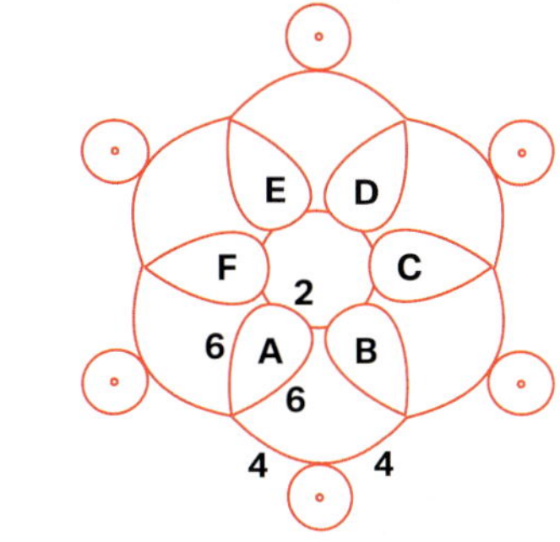

2

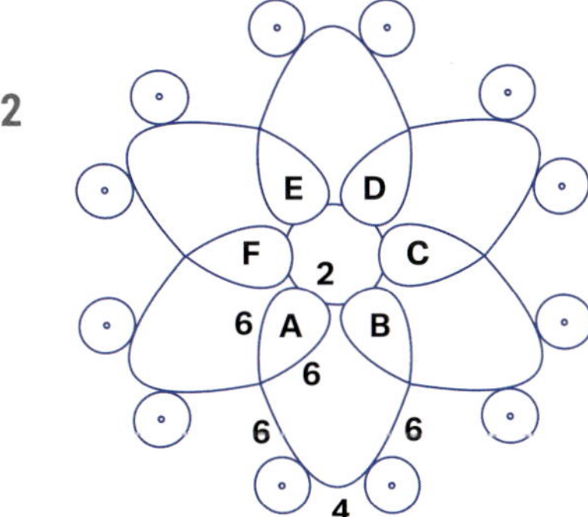

3

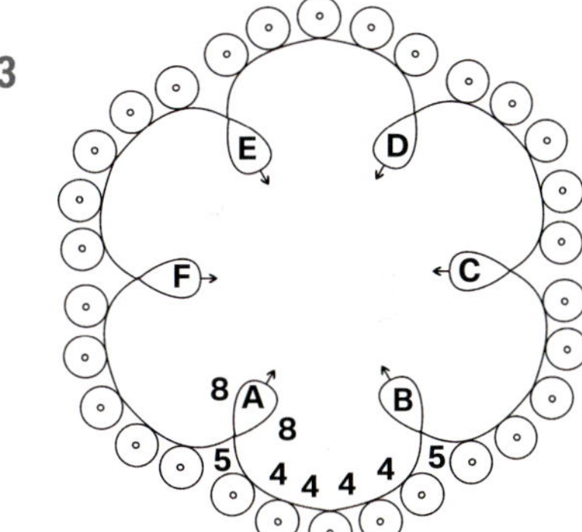

4

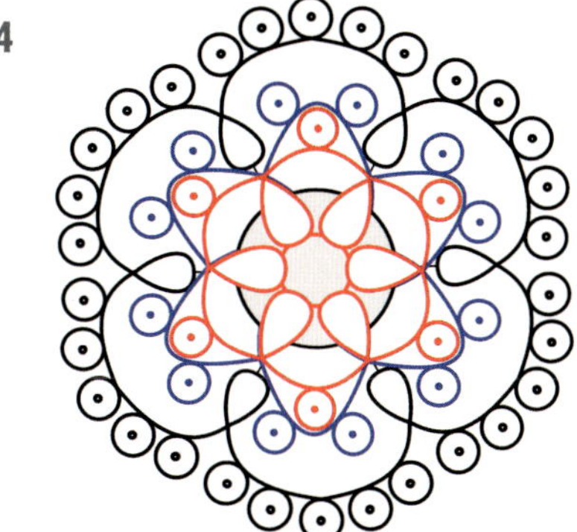

MARY

YOU WILL NEED

- Size 20 thread
- Shuttle
- Crochet hook, 0.4mm (US 16)
- 66 x size 11 beads

INSTRUCTIONS

String 54 of the beads and wind about 3.5m (3¾yd) of thread onto the shuttle with 24 beads, leaving 30 beads on the ball thread. The remaining 12 beads are added to picots before working joins, using the fine crochet hook.

R.A   (See diagram 1) 7, p, 3, p, 7, cl, RW

CH.   5, p, 5, RW

R.B   Bring 4 beads into the ring round your hand 6, 4B, 6, cl, RW

CH.   Move 1 bead up on the ball thread 8, 3B, 8, RW

R.C   (See diagram 2) 6, + to the beaded picot on ring 'B' with 1 bead to the left of the join and 3 beads to the right of the join, 6, cl, RW

CH.   Move up a bead on the ball thread 5, p, 5, RW

R.D   7, add a bead to the second picot on ring A using the crochet hook, 3, p, 7, cl, RW

1

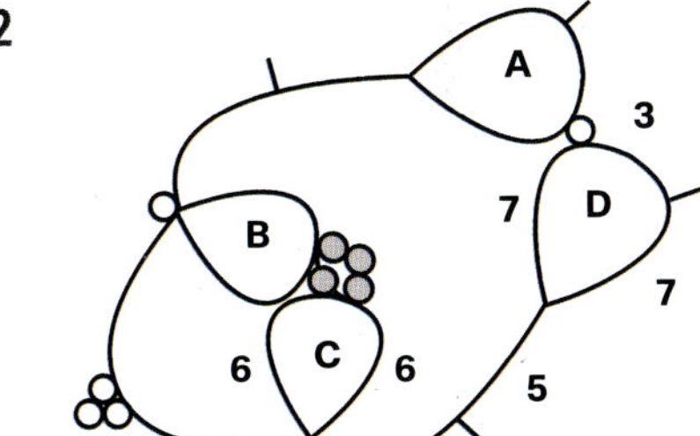

2

*CH.   (See diagram 3) 5, add a bead and join to the picot on the previous chain,
       5, RW

R.E   Bring 4 beads into the ring round your hand 6, 4B, 6, cl, RW (see diagram 3)

CH.   Move up a bead on the ball thread 8, 3B, 8, RW

R.F   6, + to the beaded picot on the previous ring with 1 bead to the left of the join
       and 3 beads to the right of the join, 6, cl, RW

CH.   Move up a bead on the ball thread 5, p, 5, RW***

R.G   7, add a bead and join to the free picot on the adjacent centre ring, 3, p, 7, cl,
       RW**

Repeat from * to ** twice more, then from * to *** once more.

R.P   (See diagram 4) 7, add a bead and join to the free picot on the adjacent centre
       ring, 3, add a bead and join to the free picot on ring A, 7, cl, RW

CH.   5, add a bead and join to the picot on the previous chain, 5, RW

R.Q   Bring 4 beads into the ring round your hand 6, 4B, 6, cl, RW

CH.   Move up a bead on the ball thread 8, 3B, 8, RW

R.R   6, + to the beaded picot on the previous ring with 1 bead to the left of the join
       and 3 beads to the right of the join, 6, cl, RW

CH.   Move up a bead on the ball thread 5, add a bead and join to the first chain, 5

Cut and tie to the base of ring A. Secure the ends. Block and stiffen as required.

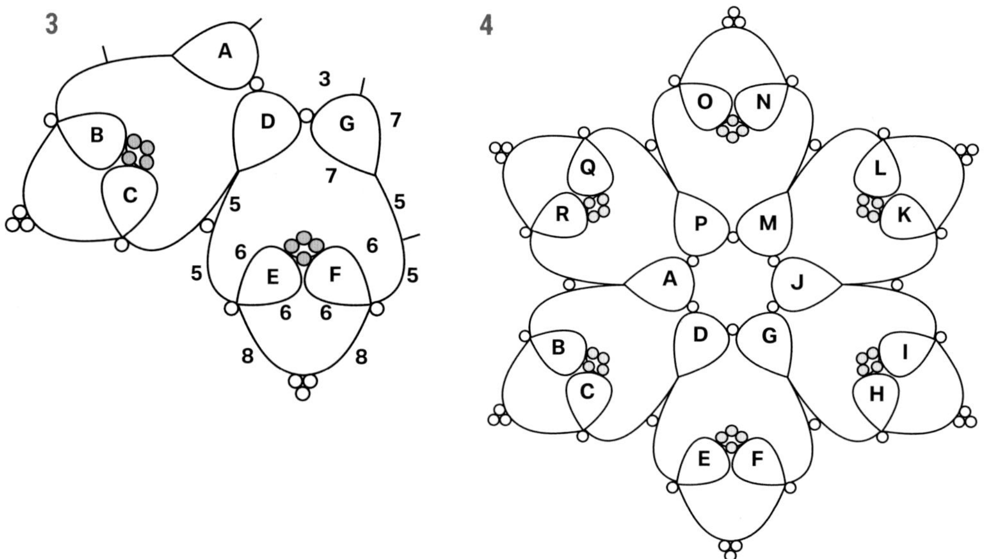

VIVIENNE

YOU WILL NEED

- Size 20 thread
- 2 x shuttles
- 2 x crochet hooks, 0.75mm and 0.4mm (US 13 and 16)
- Small pair of scissors
- Tapestry needle or beading needle
- 72 x size 11 beads

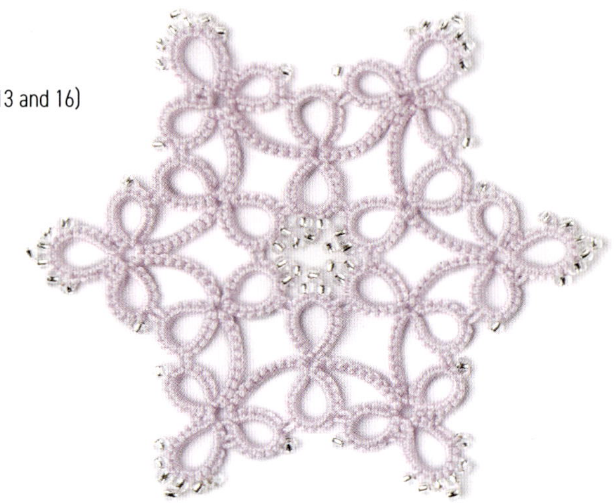

INSTRUCTIONS

String the beads then wind 2 shuttles CTM with 6m (6½yd) of thread and 54 beads onto shuttle 1 and 4m (4½yd) of thread with the remaining 18 beads onto shuttle 2.

Note: the rings shown in red in the diagrams are worked using shuttle 2.

SH.1	R.A	(See diagram 1) Bring 1 bead from shuttle 1 into the ring round your hand and work 6, p, 2, B, 6, p, 2, cl
	R.B	Bring 7 beads into the ring round your hand 2, + to previous ring, 4, B, 2, B, 2, 3B, 2, B, 2, B, 4, p, 2, cl
	R.C	Bring 1 bead into the ring round your hand 2, + to previous ring, 6, B, 2, p, 6, cl, RW (see diagram 1)
SH.1	CH.	10, RW
	R.D	6, + to previous ring, 6, p, 6, cl, RW, SS
SH.2	R.E	Bring 3 beads into the ring round your hand and work 6, p, 3, 3B, 3, p, 6, cl, DNRW, SS
SH.1	CH.	10, RW

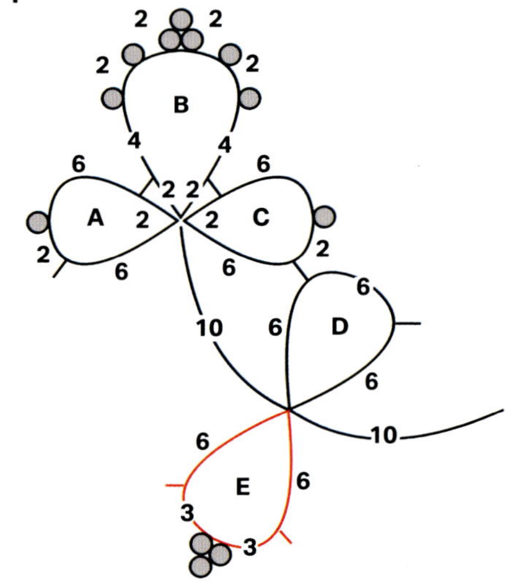

*R.F (See diagram 2) Bring 1 bead into the
      ring round your hand 6, + to ring D, 2, B,
      6, p, 2, cl

R.G   Bring 7 beads into the ring round your
      hand 2, + to previous ring, 4, B, 2, B, 2, 3B,
      2, B, 2, B, 4, p, 2, cl

R.H   Bring 1 bead into the ring round your
      hand 2, + to previous ring, 6, B, 2, p,
      6 cl, RW

CH.   10, RW

R.I   6, + to previous ring, 6, p, 6, cl, RW, SS

SH.2 R.J Bring 3 beads into the ring round
           your hand

           6, + to previous centre ring, 3, 3B, 3, p, 6,
           cl, DNRW, SS

SH.1 CH. 10, RW**

Repeat from * to ** four more times, remembering to
join ring Y to rings X and A, and to join centre ring Z to
rings U and E (see diagram 3).

Cut and tie to the base of rings A, B and C. Secure the
ends. Block and stiffen as required.

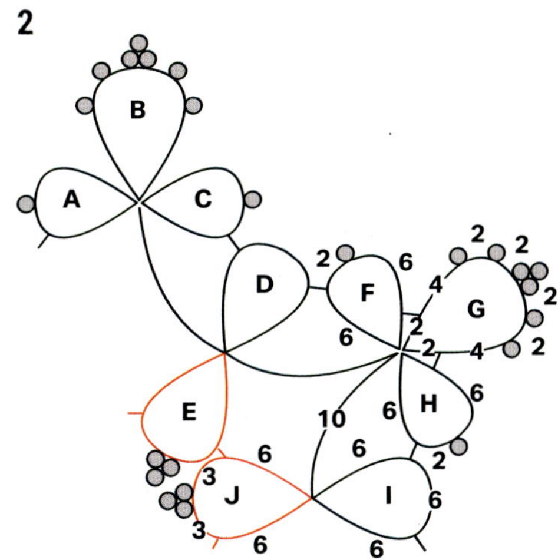

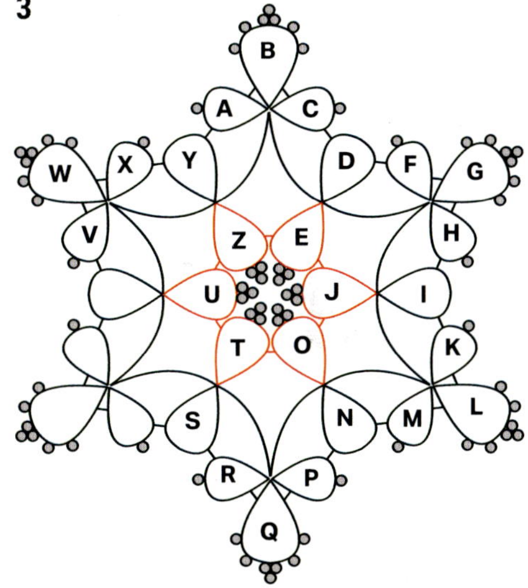

JAN

YOU WILL NEED

- Size 20 thread
- Shuttle
- Crochet hook, 0.75mm (US 13)
- Small pair of scissors

INSTRUCTIONS

Wind about 1.5m (1¾yd) of thread onto the shuttle. Do not cut.

ROW 1

R.A   6, large picot (1cm/½in), 6, cl, RW

CH.   5, p, 1, p, 1, p, 5, RW (see diagram 1)

*R.B   6, + to picot on ring A, 6, cl, RW

CH.   5, p, 1, p, 1, p, 5, RW** (see diagram 2)

Repeat from * to ** four more times but do not reverse work after the fourth repeat.

Work a shuttle join (sj) into the base of ring A (see diagram 3).

Do not cut.

ROW 2

CH.   6, mp, 2, Lp, 2, mp, 6, sj into the base of the adjacent ring

Repeat this chain five more times, omitting the final shuttle join, then cut and tie to the base of ring A (see diagram 4).

Block and stiffen as required.

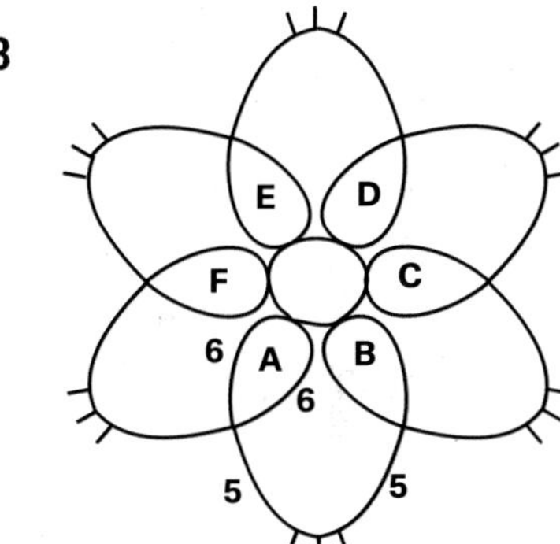

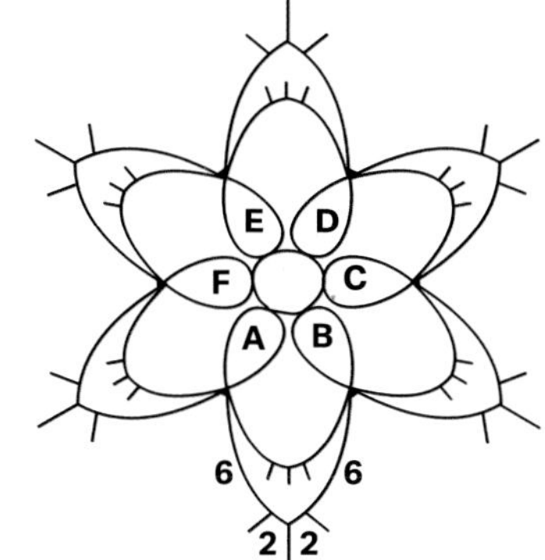

"

HANNAH

YOU WILL NEED

- Size 10 thread
- Shuttle
- Crochet hook, 0.75mm (US 13)
- Small pair of scissors
- Tapestry needle or beading needle
- 15mm (⅝in) two-hole button
- 3 x picot gauges (an unfolded paper clip for 'p', cocktail stick for 'mp' and pencil for 'vbp')

INSTRUCTIONS

Wind 1.5m (1¾yd) of thread onto the shuttle. Do not cut.

R.A	5, + to one of the holes in the button, 5, cl, RW
CH.	2, p, 2, p, 2, mp, 2, mp, 2, vbp, 2, mp, 2, mp, 2, p, 2, p, 2, tension to measure about 2.5cm (1in), RW
R.B	5, + the same hole in the button, 5, cl, RW
CH.	As above
R.C	5, + the same hole in the button, 5, cl, RW
CH.	As above
R.D	5, + the other hole in the button, 5, cl, RW
CH.	As above
R.E	5, + the same hole in the button, 5, cl, RW
CH.	As above
R.F	5, + the same hole in the button, 5, cl, RW
CH.	As above

Cut and tie to the base of ring A, then secure the ends.
Block and stiffen as required.

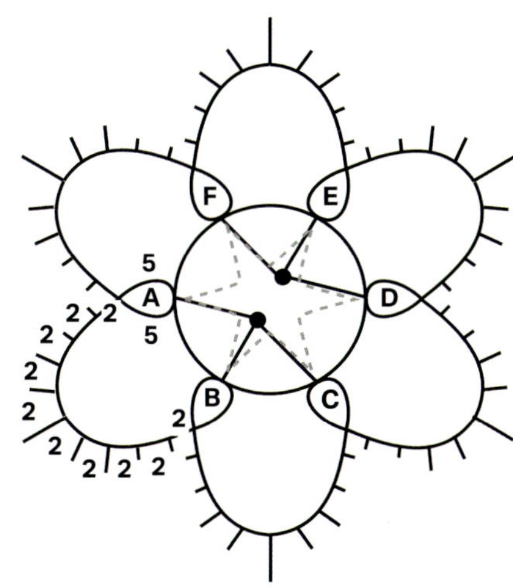

RUTH

YOU WILL NEED

- Size 20 thread
- 2 x shuttles
- Crochet hook, 0.75mm (US 13)
- Small pair of scissors
- Tapestry needle or beading needle

INSTRUCTIONS

Wind 2 shuttles CTM with about 3m (3¼yd) of thread onto shuttle 1 and 5m (5½yd) of thread onto shuttle 2.

SH.1	R.A	(See diagram 1) 8, p, 4, p, 2, p, 2, cl
	R.B	2, + to ring A, 4, p, 6, cl, RW
	CH.	12, p, 2, SS, DNRW
SH.2	R.C	2, + to previous chain, 6, mp, 6, p, 2, cl
	R.D	2, + to ring C, 6, mp, 6, p, 2, cl, SS, DNRW

SH.1 CH. 2, + to ring D, 12, RW
R.E 8, + to ring A, 4, p, 2, p, 2, cl
R.F 2, + to ring E, 4, p, 6, cl, RW
CH. 12, p, 2, SS, DNRW

SH.2 R.G 2, + to previous chain, 6, mp, 6, p, 2, cl
R.H 2, + to ring G, 6, mp, 6, p, 2, cl, SS, DNRW

SH.1 CH. (See diagram 2) 2, + to ring H, 12, RW
R.I 8, + to ring E, 4, p, 2, p, 2, cl
R.J 2, + to ring I, 4, p, 6, cl, RW
CH. 12, p, 2, SS, DNRW

SH.2 R.K 2, + to previous chain, 6, mp, 6, p, 2, cl
R.L 2, + to ring K, 6, mp, 6, p, 2, cl, SS, DNRW

SH.1 CH. 2, + to ring L, 12, RW
R.M 8, + to ring I, 4, p, 2, p, 2, cl
R.N 2, + to ring M, 4, p, 6, cl, RW
CH. 12, p, 2, SS, DNRW

SH.2 R.O 2, + to previous chain, 6, mp, 6, p, 2, cl
R.P 2, + to ring O, 6, mp, 6, p, 2, cl, SS, DNRW

SH.1 CH. 2, + to ring P, 12, RW
R.Q 8, + to ring M, 4, p, 2, p, 2, cl
R.R 2, + to ring Q, 4, p, 6, cl, RW
CH. 12, p, 2, SS, DNRW

SH.2 R.S 2, + to previous chain, 6, mp, 6, p, 2, cl
R.T 2, + to ring S, 6, mp, 6, p, 2, cl, SS, DNRW

SH.1 CH. 2, + to ring T, 12, RW
R.U 8, + to ring Q, 4, + to ring A, 2, p, 2, cl
R.V 2, + to ring U, 4, p, 6, cl, RW
CH. 12, p, 2, SS, DNRW

SH.2 R.W 2, + to previous chain, 6, mp, 6, p, 2, cl
R.X 2, + to ring W, 6, mp, 6, p, 2, cl, SS, DNRW

SH.1 CH. 2, + to ring X, 12, RW

Cut and tie to the base of rings A and B, then secure
the ends.

Block to shape the chains as in the photo, and stiffen
as required.

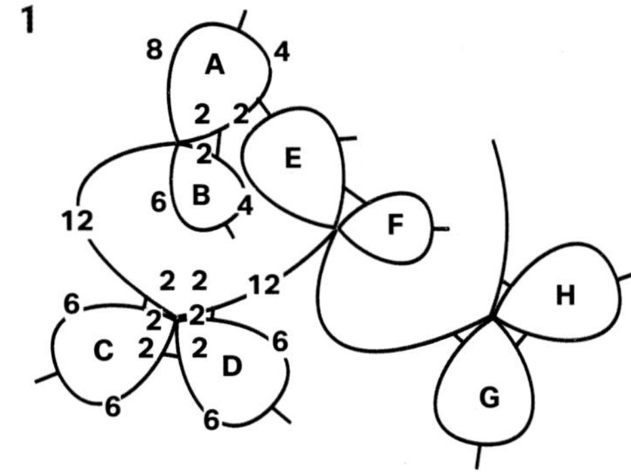

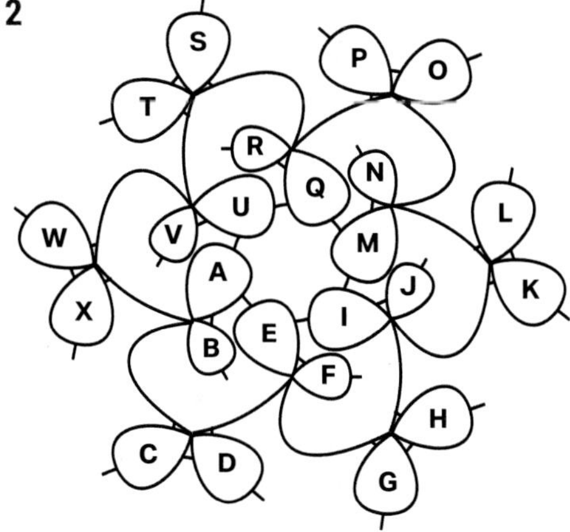

CHRISTINE

The snowflake used for the coaster shown here is Arwenna
(see pages 43–45).

YOU WILL NEED

- Size 20 thread
- Shuttle
- 2 x crochet hooks, 0.75mm and 0.4mm (US 13 and 16)
- Small pair of scissors
- Big-eyed needle or beading needle
- 48 x size 11 beads for each snowflake

INSTRUCTIONS

ROW 1

String 24 beads and wind about 0.75m (¾yd) of thread with 15 of the beads onto the shuttle, leaving 9 of the beads on the ball thread. Do not cut. Use 3 beads for all beaded dpbs.

R.A   (See diagram 1) Bring 5 beads from the shuttle into the ring round your hand, 5, B, 3, 3B, 3, B, 5, cl, RW

CH.   3, beaded dpb, 3, tension so that the dpb really curves down below the chain, RW

R.B   Bring 5 beads from the shuttle into the ring round your hand, 5, B, 3, 3B, 3, B, 5, cl, RW

CH.   3, beaded dpb, 3, tension so that the dpb really curves down below the chain, RW

R.C   Bring 5 beads from the shuttle into the ring round your hand, 5, B, 3, 3B, 3, B, 5, cl, RW

CH.   3, beaded dpb, 3, tension so that the dpb really curves down below the chain

Cut and tie to the base of ring A then secure the ends.

ROW 2

Work row 2 the same as row 1.

To assemble the snowflake, position row 2 on top of row 1 so that the 6 beaded rings are evenly spaced, then draw the beaded dropped picots of row 1 up through the centre of the snowflake so that they sit on top of the rings on row 2 (see diagram 2).

It is easier to do this if you block the snowflake by pinning the beaded dropped picots in place, then evenly space the rings before pinning them into position.

Block and stiffen as required.

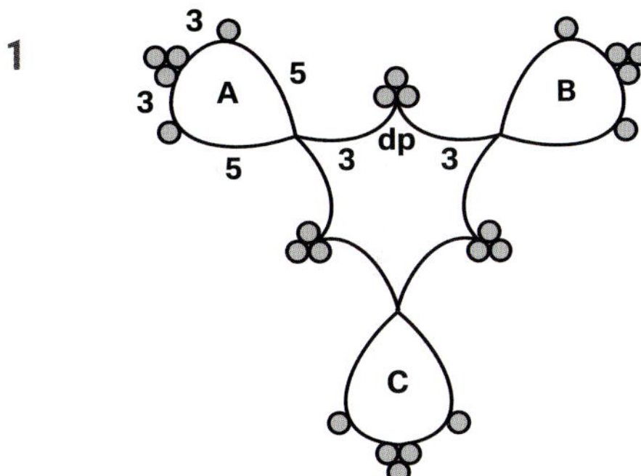

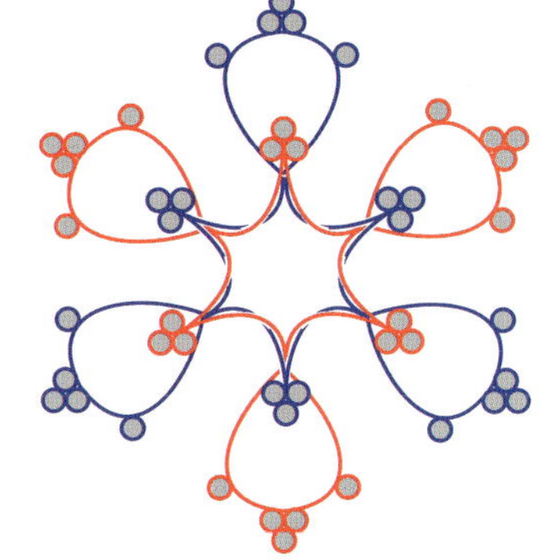

SPECIAL STITCH

Josephine ring (JR.): work a double stitch, then 12 second half stitches, close the ring.

JULIA

YOU WILL NEED

- Size 20 thread
- 2 x shuttles
- Crochet hook, 0.75mm (US 13)
- Small pair of scissors
- Tapestry needle or beading needle

INSTRUCTIONS

Wind two shuttles CTM with about 7m (7½yd) of thread on shuttle 1 and 2.5m (2¾yd) of thread on shuttle 2 (see diagram 1).

SH.2 JR.A 1, 12 second half stitches, cl, DNRW, SS (see diagram 1)

SH.1 LC. 6
        CH. 1, vsp, 2, RW
        R.B 8, p, 5, p, 3, cl, RW
        CH. 3, RW
        R.C 3, + to previous ring, 5, p, 5, p, 3, cl, RW
        CH. 3, RW
        R.D 3, + to previous ring, 5, p, 5, p, 3, cl, RW
        CH. 3, RW
        R.E 3, + to previous ring, 5, p, 5, p, 3, cl, RW
        CH. 3, RW
        R.F 3, + to previous ring, 5, p, 8, cl, RW
        CH. 2, + to vsp on the chain before ring B, 1

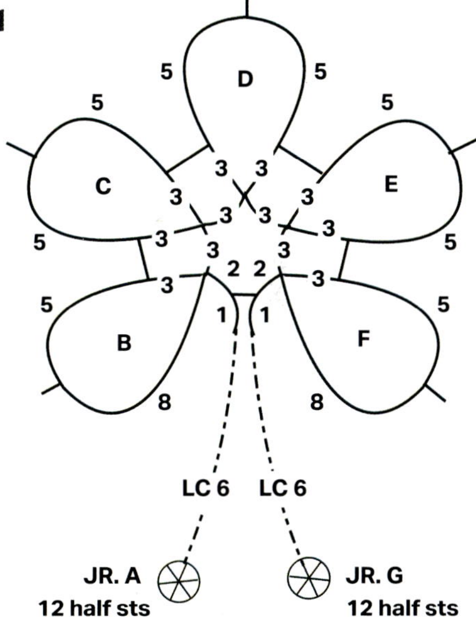

	LC.	6, DNRW, SS (see diagram 2)

*SH.2	JR.G	1, 12 second half stitches, cl, DNRW, SS

SH.1	LC.	6
	CH.	1, vsp, 2, RW
	R.H	8, + to last ring of the previous group of five rings, 5, p, 3, cl, RW
	CH.	3, RW
	R.I	3, + to previous ring, 5, p, 5, p, 3, cl, RW
	CH.	3, RW
	R.J	3, + to previous ring, 5, p, 5, p, 3, cl, RW
	CH.	3, RW
	R.K	3, + to previous ring, 5, p, 5, p, 3, cl, RW
	CH.	3, RW**
	R.L	3, + to previous ring, 5, p, 8, cl, RW
	CH.	2, + to vsp on the chain before the first ring of the five-ring group of rings, 1
	LC.	6, DNRW, SS***

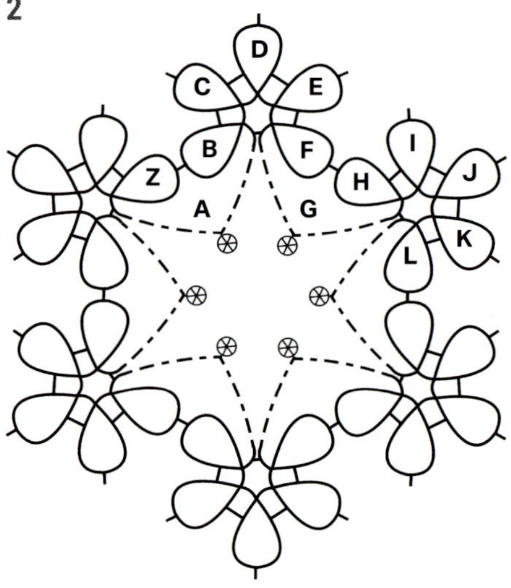

Repeat from * to *** three more times, then from * to **.

SH.1	R.Z	3, + to previous ring, 5, + to ring B, 8, cl, RW (see diagram 2)
	CH.	2, + to vsp on the chain before the first ring of the five-ring group of rings, 1
	LC.	6

Cut and tie to the base of JR.A. Block and stiffen as required.

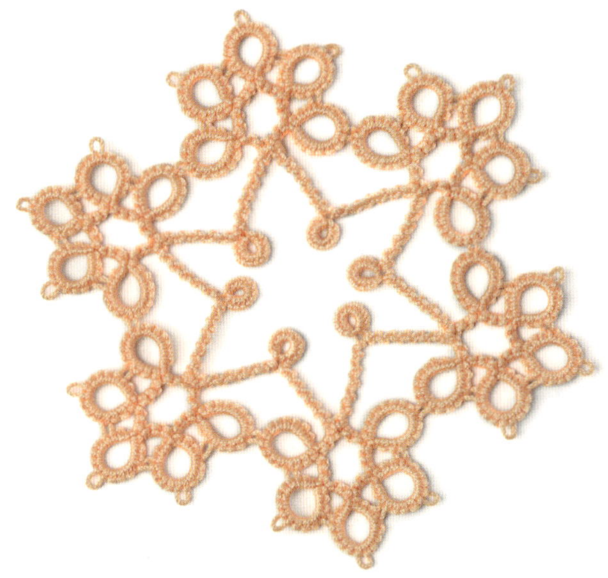

YOU WILL NEED

- Size 20 thread
- Shuttle
- 2 x crochet hooks, 0.75mm and 0.4mm (US 13 and 16)
- Small pair of scissors
- Tapestry needle or beading needle
- 6 x 1cm (½in) 4-hole buttons
- 6 x 3.4mm (⅛in) drop beads
- 3 x picot gauges (an unfolded paper clip for 'p', cocktail stick for 'mp' and pencil for 'vbp')

INSTRUCTIONS

ROW 1

Wind about 1m (1yd) of thread onto the shuttle. Do not cut.

R.A (See diagram 1) 6, p, 3, p, 6, cl, RW

CH. 7, + to a button, 7, RW

R.B 6, p, 3, p, 6, cl, RW

CH. 7, + to a different button, 7, RW

R.C (See diagram 2) 6, + to ring A, 3, p, 6, cl, RW

CH. 7, + to a different button, 7, RW

R.D 6, + to ring B, 3, p, 6, cl, RW

CH. 7, + to a different button, 7, RW

R.E 6, + to ring C, 3, + to ring A, 6, cl, RW

CH. 7, + to a different button, 7, RW

R.F 6, + to ring D, 3, + to ring B, 6, cl, RW

CH. 7, + to a different button, 7

Cut and tie to the base of ring A then secure the ends.

1

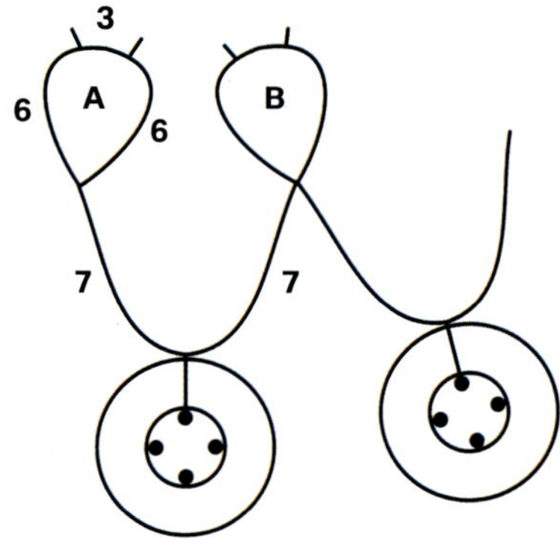

2

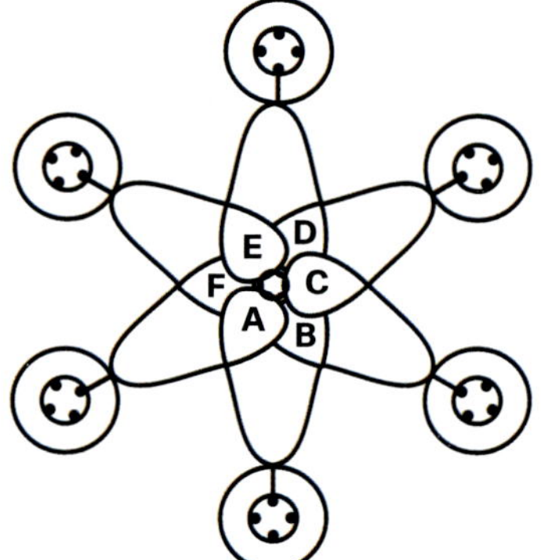

44

ROW 2 (SEE DIAGRAM 3)

String the 6 drop beads then wind about 6m (6½yd) onto the shuttle, leaving the beads on the ball thread. Do not cut (see diagram 3).

*R.A   8, + to one of the buttons making the join to the hole that is directly opposite the one that is joined to row 1, 8, cl, RW

CH.   9, p, 2, RW

R.B   8, + to the hole in the same button that is to the right of the previous join, 8, cl

R.C   8, + to the first free hole in the adjacent button on row 1, 8, cl, RW

CH.   2, + to the previous chain, 9, RW

R.D   8, + to the same button in the hole that is directly opposite the one that is joined to row 1, 8, cl, RW

CH.   9, move up the drop bead, 9, RW**

Repeat from * to ** five more times, then sj to the base of ring A and continue onto row 3 without cutting the threads.

ROW 3 (SEE DIAGRAM 3)

*CH.   2, (mp, 2) x 4, sj to the joining picot between the two chains that are before and after rings B and C on row 2

CH.   2, (mp, 2) x 4, sj to the small space at the base of ring D

CH.   2 (mp, 2) x 4, sj to the side of the drop bead

MR.   6, LP, 6, sj to the other side of the same drop bead

CH.   2, (mp, 2) x 4, sj to the small space at the base of ring E**

Repeat from * to ** five more times, then cut and tie to the start of the row and secure the ends. Block and stiffen as required.

3

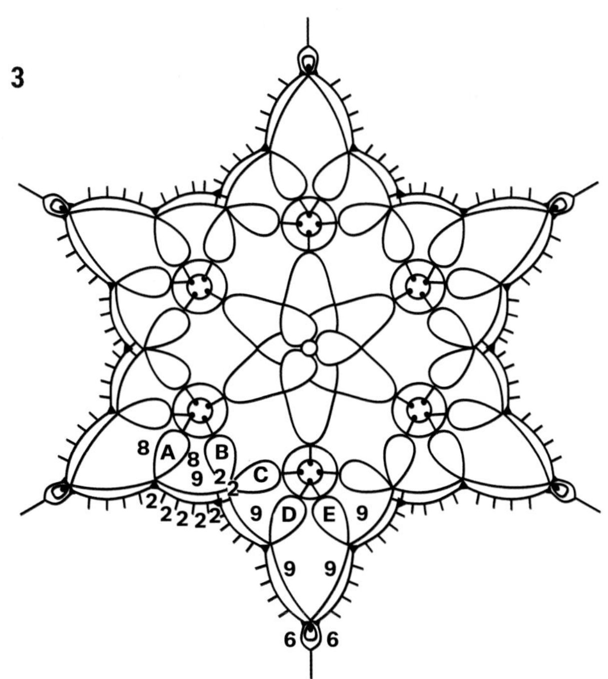

DINAH

YOU WILL NEED

- White and orange size 20 thread
- Shuttle
- Crochet hook, 0.75mm (US 13)
- Small pair of scissors
- 18 x silver and 18 x orange size 11 beads

INSTRUCTIONS

On the white thread string the beads in the following order (silver, orange, silver) x 6. Wind about 2.5m (2¾yd) of the orange thread onto the shuttle, with the beads. Loosely knot the white and orange threads together. The orange thread is the ball thread.

ROW 1

*R.   Bring 3 beads into the ring round your hand, 3, 3B, 3, vsp, 10, cl, (see diagram 1), SLT

CH.2,   p, 4, p, 1, p, 1, p, 4, p, 2, pull up the chain so that it fits snugly over the outside of the ring above the 10 ds on the ring, sj to the vsp, (see diagram 2)**

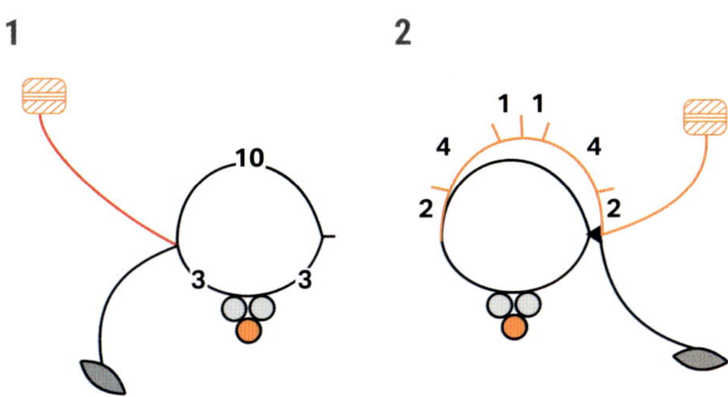

Repeat from * to ** five more times (as in diagrams 3 and 4).

Cut and tie the matching coloured threads to the start of the first ring.

ROW 2

On the white thread string the beads in the following order (orange, silver, orange) x 6. Wind about 1m (1yd) of the orange thread onto the shuttle. Knot the white and orange ends together loosely.

Work a shuttle join into the first picot on one of the chains on row 1 and into the last picot on the previous chain (just one shuttle join).

*CH.   1, LC 5, chain 1, move up 3 beads on the white thread, chain 1, LC 5, chain 1, sj to the first picot on the adjacent chain and into the last picot on the previous chain** (see diagram 5).

Repeat from * to ** five times.

Cut and tie matching coloured threads at the start of the row. Secure all the ends.

Block and stiffen as required.

3

4

5

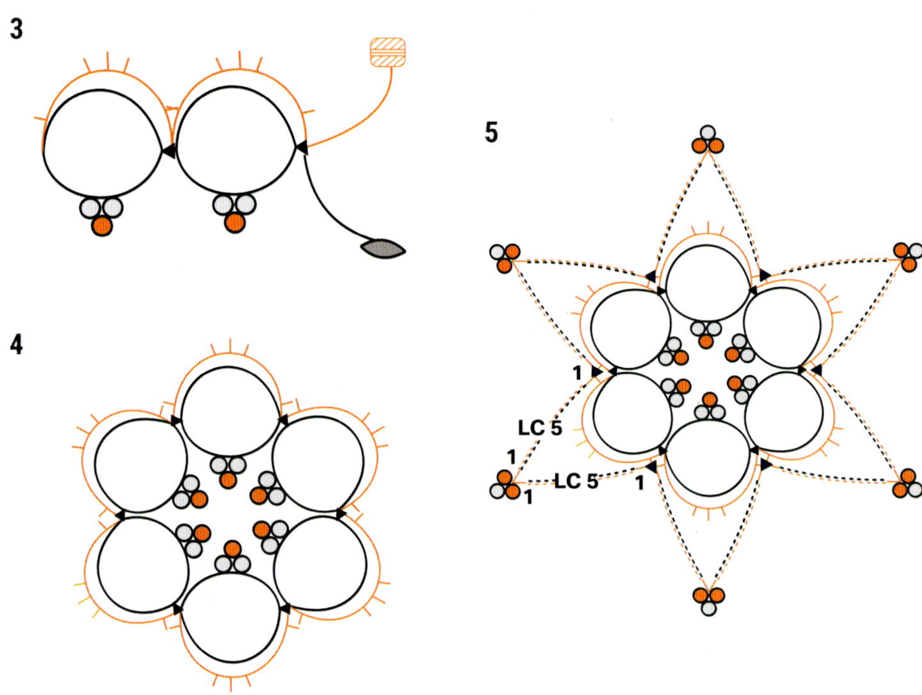

LYNN

YOU WILL NEED

- Size 20 thread
- 2 x shuttles
- Crochet hook, 0.75mm (US 13)
- Small pair of scissors
- Tapestry needle
- Small curtain ring measuring approximately 15mm (⅝in) in diameter

INSTRUCTIONS

ROW 1 (SEE DIAGRAMS 1–9)

Wind 2 shuttles CTM with about 2m (2¼yd) of thread onto shuttle 1 and 4.5m (5yd) of thread onto shuttle 2.

Using shuttle 1 (blue in diagrams 1–9), cover the curtain ring with 36 double stitches.

You might find it helpful when you are working row 2 to place a marker, such as a length of contrasting coloured thread, every 6 double stitches. Make an overhand tie with the thread from shuttle 2 at the start of the row. Do not cut.

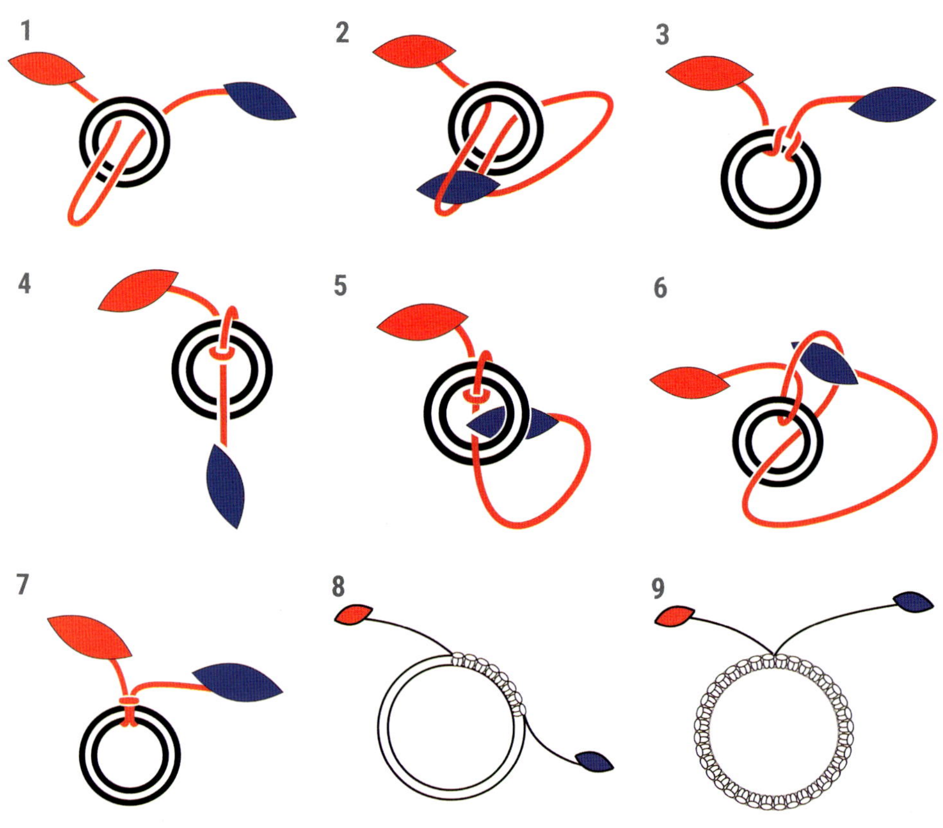

ROW 2 (SEE DIAGRAM 10)

*SH.1   CH.   4, SS, DNRW

SH.2   R.A   6, p, 3, p, 3, cl, SS, DNRW

SH.1   CH.   4, SS, DNRW

SH. 2   R.B   3, + to ring A, 3, p, 2, mp, 2, p, 3, p, 3, cl, SS, DNRW

SH.1   CH.   4, SS, DNRW

SH.2   R.C   3, + to the last picot on ring B, 3, p, 6, cl, SS, DNRW

SH.1   CH.   4, tension the chain to measure about 2cm (¾in) then miss 6 double stitches on row 1 and make a shuttle join between the sixth and seventh double stitch.**

Repeat from * to ** five more times, omitting the shuttle join at the end of the fifth repeat. Cut and tie to the start of the row then secure the ends.

Block and stiffen as required.

10

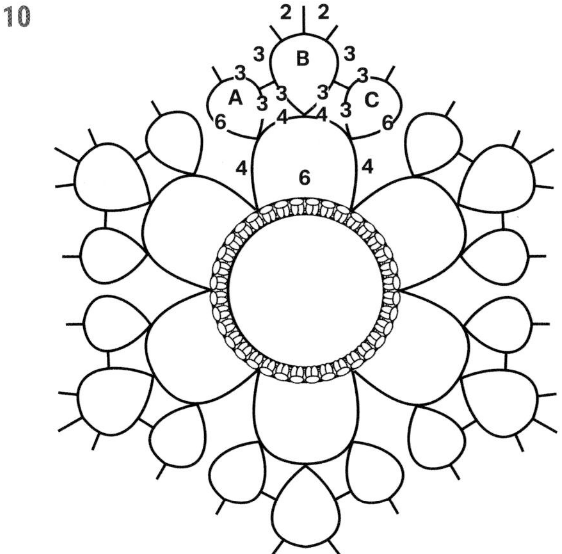

EILEEN

YOU WILL NEED

- Size 20 thread
- 2 x shuttles
- Crochet hook, 0.75mm (US 13)
- Small pair of scissors
- Tapestry needle or beading needle
- Small curtain ring measuring approximately 15mm (⅝in) in diameter
- 3 x picot gauges (an unfolded paper clip for 'p', cocktail stick for 'mp' and pencil for 'vbp')

INSTRUCTIONS

Wind 2 shuttles CTM with about 2m (2¼yd) of thread onto shuttle 1 and
2.5m (2¾yd) of thread onto shuttle 2.

ROW 1

Follow the instructions for Lynn on page 50 to cover the curtain ring with
36 double stitches (shuttle 1 = blue in diagrams 1–9). Make an overhand tie
with the thread from shuttle 2 at the start of the row. Do not cut. Continue
on to the second row.

ROW 2 (SEE DIAGRAM 1)

*SH.1   CH.   4, mp, 4, SS, DNRW

SH.2   R.   6, mp, 6, cl, SS, DNRW

SH.1   CH.   4, mp, 4, tension the chain to measure about 2cm (¾in) then
count 6 double stitches on row 1 and make a shuttle join
between the sixth and seventh double stitch.

Repeat from * five more times, omitting the shuttle join at the end of the
fifth repeat. Cut and tie to the start of the row then secure ends.

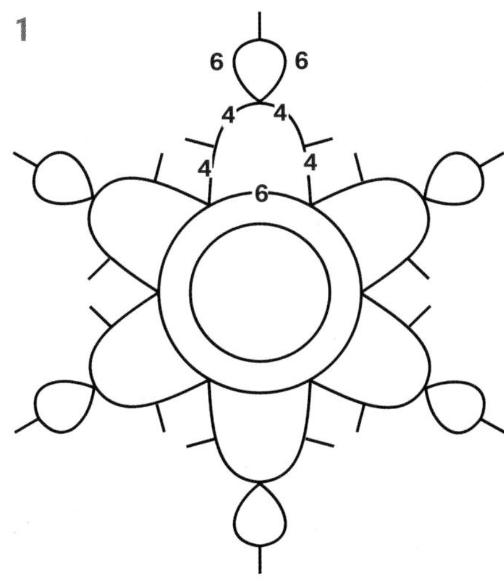

ROW 3 (SEE DIAGRAMS 2 AND 3)

Wind 2 shuttles CTM with about 4.5m (5yd) of thread onto each shuttle.

SH.1   R.A   6, + to the last picot worked on one of the chains of the second row, 2, + to the first picot worked on the adjacent chain of the second row, 6, cl, RW

        *CH. 8, RW

        R.B   6, + to the first ring on the second row, 3, p, 3, cl, RW

        CH. 10, RW

        R.C   4, + to ring B, 2, p, 4, cl, RW, SS

SH.2   R.D   6, p, 2, Lp, 2, p, 6, cl, DNRW, SS

SH.1   CH. 10, RW

        R.E   3, + to ring C, 3, + to the same ring on the second row as ring 'B', 6, cl, RW

        CH. 8, RW***

        R.F   6, + to the last picot on the same chain on the second row, 2, + to the first picot on the adjacent chain, 6, cl, RW**

Repeat from * to ** four more times, then from * to *** once
(see diagram 3).

Cut and tie to the base of the start of the row. Block and stiffen as required.

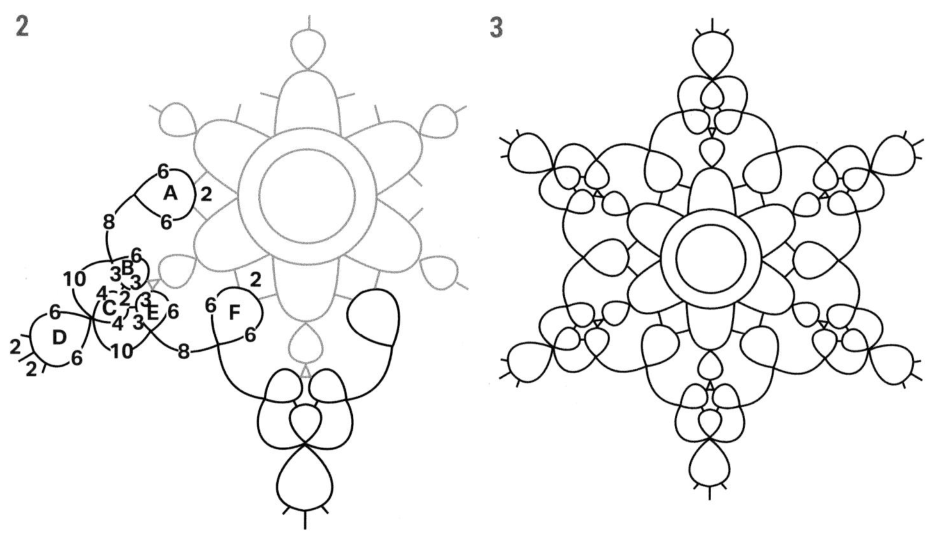

YOU WILL NEED

- Size 20 thread
- Shuttle
- Crochet hook, 0.75mm (US 13)
- Small pair of scissors
- Fine needle

- 6 x size 4mm (³⁄₁₆in) pearl beads
- 2 x jewellery finding split rings
- 2 x ear wires
- Necklace bail
- Chain necklace with clasp

INSTRUCTIONS

EARRINGS (MAKE 2)

Wind about 1m (1yd) of thread onto the shuttle. Do not cut.

R.A   3, p, 5, + to one of the jewellery finding split rings, 1, + to split ring again, 5, p, 3, cl, RW

CH.   2, RW

*R.B   3, + to previous ring, 5, mp, 5, p, 3, cl, RW (see diagram 1)

CH.   2, RW**

Repeat from * to ** three more times, then continue:

R.F   3, + to previous ring, 5, mp, 5, + to ring A (using the folded join technique on page 11), 3, cl, RW

CH.   2

Cut, leaving ends about 15cm (6in) and tie to the base of ring A.

Using the fine needle, take both threads through the 4mm (³⁄₁₆in) bead and tie them to the base of ring D. Secure the ends (see diagram 2).

Work the second earring, then block and stiffen the motifs as required. Attach an ear wire to each jewellery finding split ring.

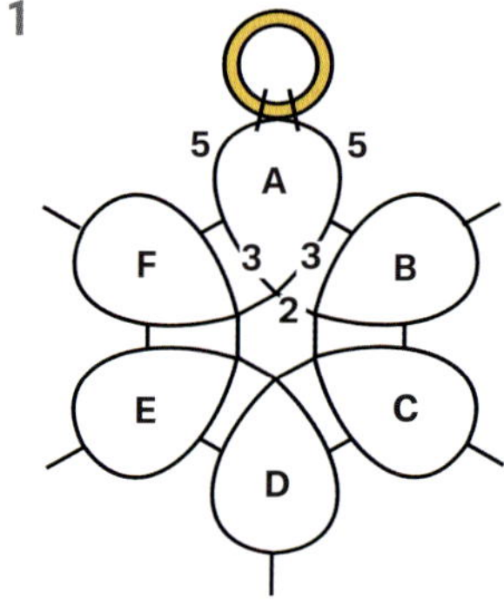

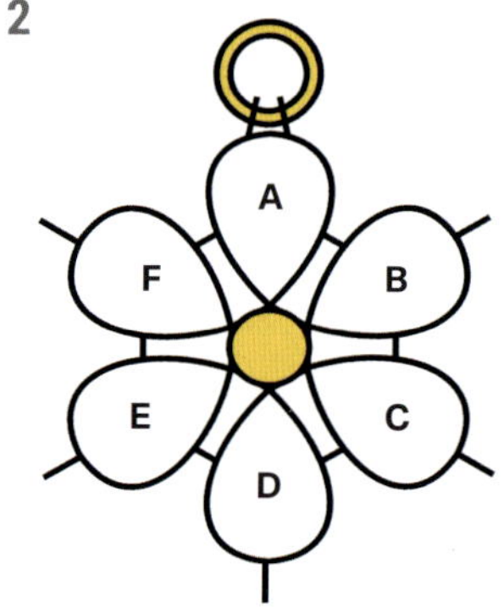

PENDANT

FIRST SNOWFLAKE MOTIF

Wind about 1m (1yd) of thread onto the shuttle.
Do not cut.

R.A   3, p, 5, + to the necklace bail (see diagram 3), 1, + to the necklace bail again, 5, p, 3, cl, RW

CH.   2, RW

Complete the first snowflake motif as for the earring snowflake motif.

SECOND SNOWFLAKE MOTIF

R.G   3, p, 5, + to ring E of first snowflake (see diagram 3), 5, p, 3, cl, RW

CH.   2, RW

R.H   3, + to ring G, 5, + to ring D of first snowflake, 5, p, 3, cl, RW

CH.   2, RW

Complete the snowflake motif by following the instructions for rings C, D, E, F on the first motif.

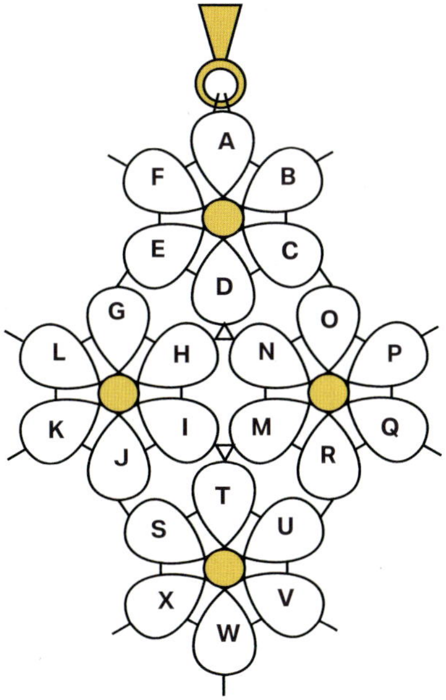

THIRD SNOWFLAKE MOTIF

R.M   3, p, 5 + to ring I on second motif, 5, p, 3, cl, RW

CH.   2, RW

R.N   3, + to ring M, 5, + to ring D on first snowflake, 5, p, 3, cl, RW

CH.   2, RW

R.O   3, + to ring N, 5, + to ring C on first snowflake, 5, p, 3, cl, RW

CH.   2, RW

Complete the snowflake motif as before (see diagram 3).

FOURTH SNOWFLAKE MOTIF

R.S   3, p, 5, + to ring J on the second snowflake, 5, p, 3, cl, RW

CH.   2, RW

R.T   3, + to ring S, 5, + to ring I on the second snowflake, 5, p, 3, cl, RW

CH.   2, RW

R.U   3, + to ring T, 5, + to ring R on the third snowflake, 5, p, 3, cl, RW

CH.   2, RW

Complete the snowflake motif as before (see diagram 3). Block and stiffen as required.

3

ANNE

YOU WILL NEED

- Size 20 thread
- 2 x shuttles
- 2 x crochet hooks, 0.75mm and 0.4mm (US 13 and 16)
- Small pair of scissors
- Tapestry needle or beading needle
- Fine needle
- 2cm (¾in) diameter sequin
- 36 x size 11 beads

INSTRUCTIONS

ROW 1

String 18 of the beads then wind about 2m (2¼yd) of thread onto the shuttle, leaving the beads on the ball thread. Do not cut (see diagram 1).

R.A   4, p, 4, p, 4, cl, RW

CH.   5, B, 5, RW

*R.B   4, + to previous ring, 4, p, 4, cl, RW

CH.   5, B, 5, RW

Repeat from * three more times, then:

R.F   4, + to previous ring, 4, + to ring A, 4, cl, RW

CH.   5, B, 5 sj to the base of ring A, RW

Do not cut, continue on to row 2.

ROW 2 (SEE DIAGRAM 2)

R.G   4, p, 4, p, 4, cl, RW

CH.   4, B, 3, p, 3, B, 4, RW

*R.H   4, + to previous ring, 4, p, 4, cl, RW

CH.   4, B, 3, p, 3, B, 4, RW

Repeat from * three more times, then:

R.L   4, + to previous ring, 4, + to ring G, 4, cl, RW

CH.   4, B, 3, p, 3, B, 4

Cut and tie to the base of ring G, then secure the ends.

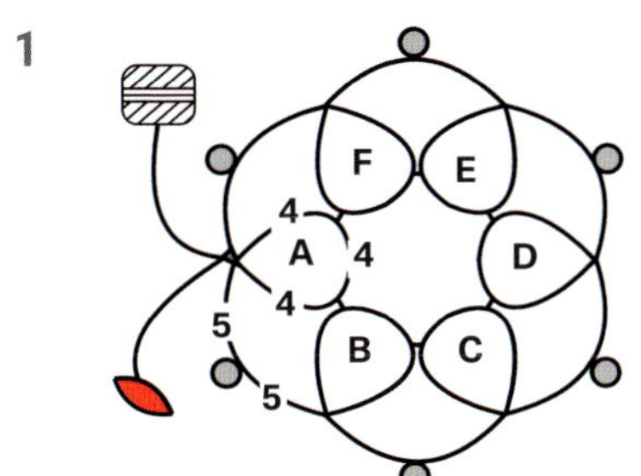

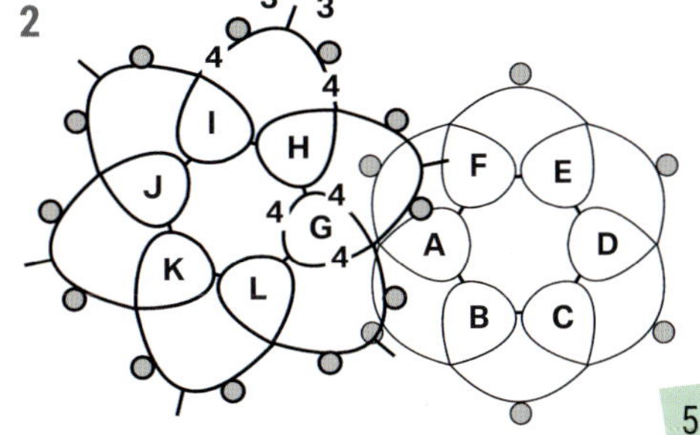

ROW 3 (SEE DIAGRAM 3)

String 18 beads then wind about 1.5m (1⅝yd) of thread onto the shuttle, leaving the beads on the ball thread. Do not cut.

Fold row 1 on top of row 2, matching up the rings. Use 3 beads for all beaded dpbs.

R.M 4, + through the base of one of the rings on row 1 and to the base of the corresponding ring on row 2 together, 4, cl, RW

CH. 8, sj to the picot on the adjacent chain on row 2

MR.N 8, beaded dpb, 8, tension then sj to the same picot

CH. 8, RW

*R.O 4, + to the base of the adjacent rings on rows 1 and 2, 4, cl, RW

CH. 8, sj to the picot on the adjacent chain on row 2

MR.P 8, beaded dpb, 8, tension then sj to the same picot

CH. 8, RW

Repeat from * twice more, slip the large sequin between rows 1 and 2 then work two more repeats to complete the row. Cut and tie then secure the ends. Block and stiffen as required.

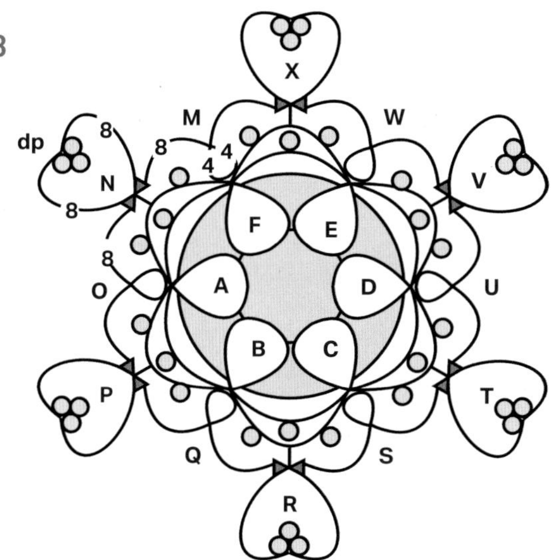

# SARAH

YOU WILL NEED

- Size 10 or 20 thread
- Shuttle
- 2 x crochet hooks, 0.75mm and 0.4mm (US 13 and 16)
- Small pair of scissors
- Tapestry needle or beading needle
- Fine needle
- 12 x 3.4mm (⅛in) drop beads

INSTRUCTIONS

Use 1 bead for all beaded dpb and beaded dpfs.

ROW 1 (SEE DIAGRAM 1)

String 6 of the drop beads then wind about 2m (2¼yd) of thread onto the shuttle, leaving the beads on the ball thread. Do not cut.

R.A   5, p, 8, p, 8, p, 5, cl, RW

CH.   Work a beaded dpb, tension to 'encourage' into place, RW

*R.B   5, + to previous ring, 8, p, 8, p, 5, cl, RW

CH.   Work a beaded dpb, tension to 'encourage' into place, RW

Repeat from * three more times, then:

R.F   5, + to previous ring, 8, p, 8, + to ring A, 5, cl, RW

CH.   Work a beaded dpb, tension to 'encourage' into place

Cut and tie to the base of ring A then secure the ends.

1

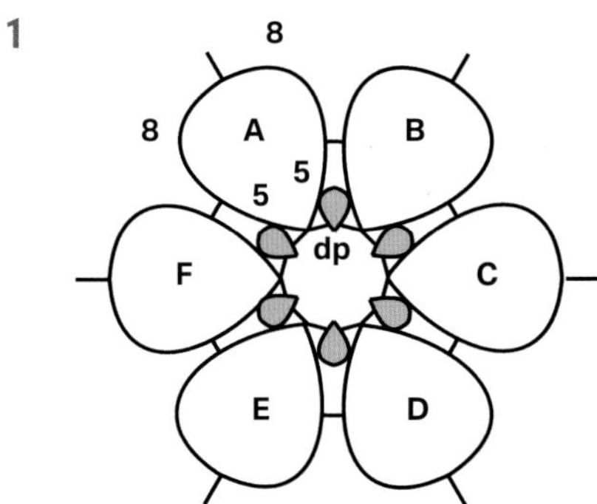

ROW 2 (SEE DIAGRAM 2)

String 6 drop beads then wind about 0.5m (½yd) of thread onto the shuttle, leaving the beads on the ball thread. Do not cut.

Join the thread to the picot between two of the rings on row 1.

*CH. 3, (p, 2) x 2, p, 1, beaded dpf, 1, (p, 2) x 2, p, 3, sj to the picot between the adjacent rings on row 1, tensioning the chain so that it sits just outside the ring

Repeat from * five more times omitting the final sj. Cut and tie to the start of the row.

ROW 3 (SEE DIAGRAMS 3 AND 4)

Wind approximately 0.75m (¾yd) of thread onto the shuttle. Do not cut.

Join to the free picot on one of the rings on row 1.

Fold the chains to the front as you work this row.

*CH. 3, (p, 2) x 3, p, 1, vbp, 1, (p, 2) x 3, p, 3, tension to curve as in the picture then sj to the free picot on the adjacent ring on row 1

Repeat from * five more times omitting the final sj. Cut and tie to the start of the row.

The chains of row 2 can be pulled forward a bit to give the snowflake a slightly 3D effect.

Block and stiffen as required.

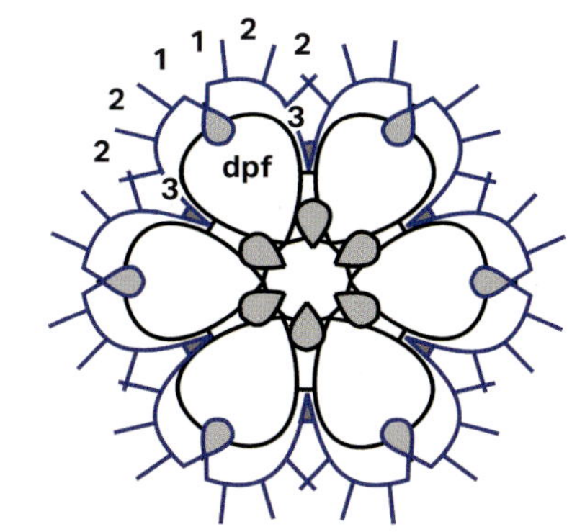

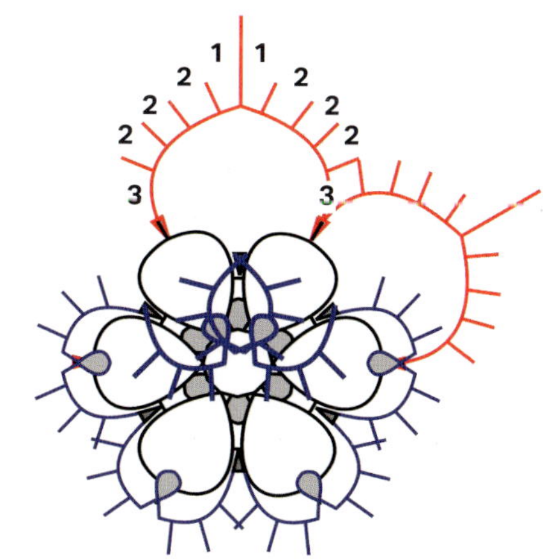

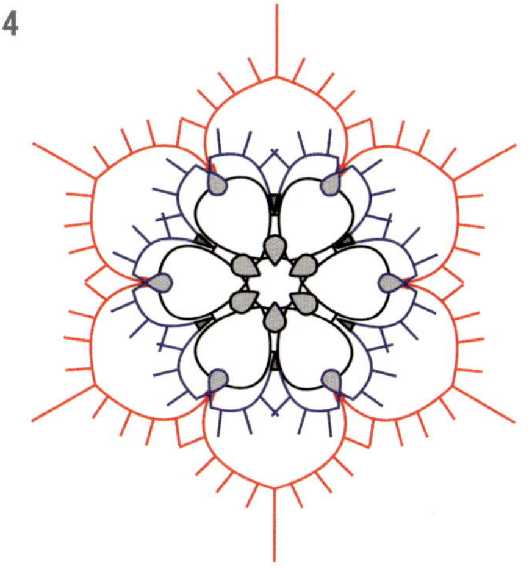

ACKNOWLEDGEMENTS

My special thanks to Hannah Crowle for proof tatting my designs and to May Corfield and the team at Search Press for enabling me to produce this book.